MONUMENTS OF MUSIC AND MUSIC LITERATURE

IN

FACSIMILE

Second Series—Music Literature

XVI

THE
PRESENT
PRACTICE OF MUSICK
VINDICATED

Matthew Locke

THE
PRESENT
PRACTICE of MUSICK
VINDICATED

A Facsimile of the London, 1673 Edition

BROUDE BROTHERS LIMITED
NEW YORK

ISBN 0-8450-2216-4

Printed in U.S.A., 1974

The Present Practice

O F

MUSICK

VINDICATED

Againſt the *Exceptions* and *New Way* of
Attaining MUSICK
Lately Publiſh'd by *Thomas Salmon*, M. A. *&c.*

By *MATTHEW LOCKE*,
Compoſer in Ordinary to His Majeſty, and Organiſt
of Her Majeſties Chappel.

To which is added
DVELLVM MVSICVM
By JOHN PHILLIPS, Gent.

Together with
A LETTER from *John Playford* to Mr. *T. Salmon*
by way of Confutation of his *Eſſay*, *&c.*

Martial Lib. 3. 67.
Iraſci noſtro non debes, Cerdo, libello,
Ars tua, non vita, eſt carmine læſa meo.
Innocuos permitte ſales. Cur ludere nobis
Non liceat, licuit ſi jugulare tibi?

London,Printed for *N. Brooke* at the *Angel* in *Cornhill*,
and *J Playford* near the *Temple-Church*. 1673.

To the Reader.

THough I may without scruple aver, that nothing has done Mr. *Salmon* more kindness, than that his Books have had the honour to be answered; yet have I been forc'd to afford him this favour, rather to chastize the Reproaches which he hath thrown upon the most Eminent Professors of Musick, than for any thing of Learning that I found in him. Those Gentlemen he accus'd of Ignorance, for not imbracing his illiterate Absurdities; for which it was necessary to bring him to the *Bar* of *Reason*, and to do him that Justice which his Follies merited. Though for the fame he gets by this I shall not much envy him; with whom it will fare, as with common Criminals, who are seldome talkt of above two or three days after Execution. The Gentleman might have slept in a whole skin, had he not challeng'd all the World; in which, how well he has behav'd himself, you may, if you please, in reading judge; and so farewel.

M. L.

To my FRIEND
Mr. *MATTHEW LOCKE*,
On his ingenious Discovery of those
MUSICAL INNOVATIONS
Held forth by the *Author* of
An Essay to the Advancement of Musick, &c.

A S MARSYAS, *though by* MINERVA *taught*,
While with insipid Novelties *he thought*,
Great PHOEBUS *of his* Lustre *to deprive*,
Was for his bold presumption *Flead alive*:
So while our LOCKE *th'* APOLLO *of our Age*,
This MUSICAL PHANATICK *doth engage*;
He both o'recomes *and* punishes *his* Pride;
Though he Flea's *not his* Skin, *he* Tawes *his* Hide.

J. Phillips.

A LETTER of THANKS

To Mr. THOMAS SALMON

For the Vindication of his Essay, *&c.*

SIR,

TO the Favours formerly acknowledged by me, and since repeated by you, you have obligingly added in the *Vindication* of your *Essay* so many others (though of far different Nature to them, yet doubtless with the same, if not greater heartiness) that I was at a loss how to put my self into the least Capacity of manifesting the thankfulness they deserve, without looking back, and endeavouring (if possible) to find out their true Rise; wherein if I fail, I shall willingly acknowledge my fault, and beg your pardon.

Sir, In your *Essay* (*pag.* 10.) you are pleas'd to affirm, *That the dark and tedious Principles of Musick, the bugbear Terms and confused Cliffs, hindred the access to it. Pag.* 11. *That the long discourse of Gibberish, a fardle of hard Names and fictitious Words, call'd the* Gam-ut, *to be learn'd backwards and forwards by heart, as though a Man must*

A   *be* be *exact in the Art of Conjuring before he learn'd Musick, terrified the Beginner.* Pag. 15. *That you cann't tell any thing that perswades Musick-Masters to trouble their Scholars with an impertinent difficulty, but a pernicious humour in some Men still to do what hath once been done, howsoever useless and unprofitable; and that though the* Gam-vt *be retain'd, they think it insufficient.* Pag. 16. *That they are to be blamed for not beginning the Naming of their Notes with* Mi. Pag. 19. *That intollerable perplexity which arose from the Alteration of the Cliffs, caus'd some charitable but lazy Wit, to invent* Tablature, *whereby the Notes are Mechanically clouded in Letters, and so darkly, that the most quick sighted Musick-Master cann't tell what they mean, till he find out the Tuning, and the Scholar, so instructed, condemn'd ever to be ignorant of the rational part of his Musick,* &c. *for the Voyce and Instruments, not capable of that literal Expression, People learn by rote, and quickly forget what like Parrots they ignorantly prated.* Pag. 22. *A Musick-Master cann't trust to the Observation of Intervals in passing from one Cliff to another.* Pag. 24. *Musick-Masters will be loath to consent to a Way, wherein every young Practitioner may rival them.* Pag. 25, 26. *Some Musick-Masters return'd me such Objections, as betray'd their misapprehension of my design, and their unwillingness it should come into practice; upon which account I have put my self to the trouble of writing these Papers, that they might the more clearly perceive the conveniency of our* Hypothesis: *And if afterwards they should remain peevish, and obstinate against the use of it, their*

Scholars

*Scholars might be able to right themselves, and de-
mand a remission of more than half their slavish
Task, for to learn the* Notes *and con their places, is
the very drudgery of Musick, &c.* which, *when once
Men find it will save them half the trouble, they
will embrace it as readily, as if I were Emperour of
the World to command it. Pag. 27. But if after
all this, Musick-Masters shall double the time in
teaching their Scholars, in hopes of double Gain ; or
their Scholars be such Fools to undergo that expence
of time and trouble; give me leave to laugh, and
let them have their labour for their pains. Pag. 32.
I will make a wild Comparison to shew how madly
Custom perswades Musicians to reckon. Pag. 36.
By how much Musicians have been wanton in their
various Cliffs for Singing, they bring in Evidence
of the Mischief it makes. Pag. 47, 48. I should
think this unworthy my pains, unless the difficulty
were so great which demands redress, and necessity
required me to answer the perverse obstinacy of some,
who would oppose even the justest Alterations ;* Vitio
malignitatis humanæ vetera semper in laude, præ-
sentia in fastigio esse. *But if any shall contemn this
because Easie and Natural, let them remember what
a grave company of such Contemners were baffled
in setting an Egg upright, till they were shewed
how. Pag. 74. If there be a nearer and an easier
way* (than the Old Scale) *why should not those Guides
be so honest to lead us in it ? &c. Truely if Musick-Masters will continue obstinate, to maintain such
needless difficulties, they may like some (Musicians) be left to play by themselves in Fidlers Island.
Pag. 78. Pity me ye* confounded Sons of *Nimrod,*

that

that I muſt ſtill ſuffer the Curſe of my old confu-
ſed diſorders. *Pag.* 88. *I have heard many Scholars in vain importune their Maſters for ſome Directions to this purpoſe (viz.* to Play or Compoſe an
Air or Conſort) *whoſe Charity notwithſtanding has
been ſo ſtraight , or elſe their Ignorance ſo obſtinate,
that their juſt intreaties were fruſtrated.* For which
Pag. 90. *Now a Maſter is ranked in the ſame order
with thoſe Empyrical Traders , who have a parcel
of Muſical Receipts , but underſtand not one Note of
their Compoſure.*

Theſe , Sir , Theſe bold and untrue Aſperſions
thrown on All Maſters of Practical Muſick , and
All Gentlemen and others that have learn'd *their
way* , as if your taking a Degree had authorized
you to abuſe Men ; together with the perpetual
magnifying your ſelf, and the Brat your *Eſſay*, were
the Motives of my inſerting a Merry Proverb or
Simily here and there in my *Obſervations* ; and
thoſe if I miſtake not of your doubty manner of
Vindicating it.

Sir , I have been told , that Generoſity is a con-
ſtant Attendant on Noble and Heroick Spirits , and
ſhould have believ'd it, had I not heard of many
Great Ones that abhorr'd the ſound of the very
word ; but you, Sir, by thoſe ſhowers of Bounty
heap'd on me in the *Vindication* of your *Eſſay*, have
made ſo abſolute a Convert of me , that I hold it a
Duty neceſſary to let the World know, how admi-
rably your Tongue ſpeaks your Heart. Sir, you
have prevented a long Journey and much trouble
for its diſcovery in your Title Page, by ſlily con-
cealing the Titles of thoſe real Favours their Majeſties

jefties have been gracioufly pleas'd to confer on me
in both their Services, that thereby you might take
advantage to render me contemptible to all that
know me not, and all other your tender-hearted
Profelites, who believe you are already in poffeffion
of fome Infallible Chair, and confequently can fpeak
or write nothing but Truth : As fair an Introduction
for your following Difcourfe as Heart could with!
In your Advice to the Reader, you tell him *Moor-
fields* and the *Bear-Garden* are Entertainments only
for the Rabble, *your old Cronies*; to prevent therefore my being drawn into the Lifts of their Active
and Martial Atchievements, you, to render me impudent as well as ignorant, have plac'd me on the
Grand Theatre of the World, bidding Defiance,
firft, to your Learned Patron Dr. *Wallis* ; then, to the
Royal Society and all *Mathematicians* that have been,
are, or fhall be ; andlaftly, to Modefty, Honefty, Piety,
and whatever elfe relates to God or Good Men.

Behold, Sir, an Abbreviate of your tranfcendent
additional Favours ! Favours indeed ! and when really confidered, fuch as in all probability could not
proceed from any but your felf, your Epiftoler,
or that Great Prince who pretends Right to all that's
donable in this World.

But of their Particulars hereafter. At prefent
give me leave, if you pleafe, to admire that fo much
Prodigality fhould be ufed to fo little purpofe ;
efpecially when I reflect on that great and extraordinary Call which neceffitated you (as your felf
confefs) to this Act of Reformation: for no
fooner can I caft my Eye on the *Vindication*, but I
lofe the *Effay*; this propofing a nearer and eafier

A 3   way

way to the attaining of Practical Mufick; that running quite from it to what either we have already paft, or to what is meerly fpeculative, or at moft infignificant to us: So that upon a true account, when your jingling with, and playing on my words, with your perpetual wrefting or falfifying them, are laid afide, there's not one word in the *Vindication* makes good the Title and Contents of the *Effay*, but your own bare affirming you have demonftrated it; which how true it is, I appeal to all Mafters of Practical Mufick, who are, and ought to be Judges in this Cafe of Practice.

Yet, Sir, left your *Whirligig Members* fhould think me too fevere, and judge that I write rather out of fpite and malice to your Perfon, than againft your Opinion (which you and your Dearly Beloved have already proclam'd, though Heaven knows for what!) be pleas'd to remember, that from *Pag.* 10. to *Pag.* 27. in my *Obfervations*, I demonftrate, *by the Old Scale, by the brief Explanation of it, and by the feveral Examples there inferted*, the Conveniency and Neceffity of the Cliffs, as they are univerfally received, *on the one fide*; and the intricacy and perplexity which perpetually attends your B M T's mutability (without which you cannot advantagioufly write any thing according to your own Rule that has the extent of a well-defign'd Compofition) *on the other.* But what's your Anfwer to this? not one word, *though it be the Hinge on which the whole Difcourfe depends, as to Practical Mufick, and which was your Task*; but (after a long Digreffion from it, intermix'd with all kind of abufive Language) an old

ftoln

stoln **Cycle**, to tell us, an *Octave* is an *Octave*, that *Musick* is part of the *Mathematicks*, which no Man yet ever doubted of that pretended to Musick ; and an Argument (if any one will take it for such) back'd with such a Scheme, as being truly applied, undeniably destroys all you pretend to build, and confirms what so furiously you would destroy ; notwithstanding your desperate threatning *to pull down* (Sampson-like) *the Observer in your ruin, and crush him with five times the weight of his own Objection :* For, those absurdities which you charge the Old Scale with, are really none, but evident Fortifiers of its certainty ; being that where-ever the *C sol fa ut Cliff* is placed, the second Space below is perpetually *G sol re ut.*

Example.

And that *one* absurdity, which you confess to be in your New Way, by the assistances of your Lieger Line and Exoticks, multiplies on every Note throughout your whole Scale.

Example.

Or thus :

This, Sir, is so evident in it self, that it needs neither Argument nor Scheme to maintain or demonstrate it to any Person indued with Common Sense. And truly, Sir, according to this Rate, this excellent Method of Proving, you may Write and Answer Books, with as much ease as you pretend you could Command the World; for nothing can come amiss to so great a Mind; the Examples of ruin'd Monarchs touch you not; the Infamy attending Libellous Scriblers holds not your hands; what you will, must be; what not, not: And this is that, and only that, which I can any way perceive the World is ever like to have from you, excepting your new invented *Wheel of Seven Spokes* for a Tyler or Carpenter to reach the top of a House with, instead of his old Ladder; your New Way of Account, to tell a Farmer *Paul*'s Fair will be *D* in the fourth *Octave*, instead of the Twenty fifth of *January*; and the incomparable B M T for a fair Lady to Learn (with all Expedition) the singing of a *Base* in Consort: which Posterity may admire you for, though the present Age be not so good natur'd. But to proceed :

In

In my *Obfervations* (*Pag.* 33. & 34.) I mention the ridiculoufnefs of confining the *Viol* to a Tuning, incapable of being ufed well in more than one Key, whereas the Old Way injoyed all ; and particularly do manifeft your contradicting your own Rule *of keeping every Octave and Part within the Syftem of Four Lines*, by planting the firft Note of an Example taken from Mr. *Simpfon* in a Sixth Line, and putting the fame Note that is to be Plaid on the fame String and Fret, here in the Line, there in the Space, then again in the Line, after that in the Space, and fo forward to the End of the Leffon. This, Sir, to any Mans thinking might have deferv'd fome Anfwer ! but 'tis put off with a bare imploying your Conjuring Exoticks, and telling the World I underftand not the *Viol* ; which how true 'tis, and how much to your pretended relieving the Hand, Eye, and Underftanding from thofe troublefome and needlefs perplexities you charge the Old Scale and Tuning with, I leave to your felf to judge ; being very much affured, that if you are infenfible of the non-performance of what you have fo boldly undertook, you are unfit to be taken farther notice of than as *an unskilful impertinent Wrangler*. But, Sir, whether I do or do not underftand the *Viol*, it matters not ; 'tis evident I did not abufe your Publifher in afferting *(ibid.)* *that he knew the impoffibility of it*. And that you may do fo to if you pleafe, take for an Experiment the following Example ; and when you have tried it the Old Tuning, apply it to your New-call'd *Univerfal One*, as in the firft Example in the following Page.

Example.

First Example for the Violl

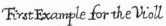

An Entry. The Second Example for the Harpsicord

This, Sir, though you are refolv'd not to be Confuted, may at long run Convince you, that I do underftand the *Viol*; that 'tis impoffible to perform it on your new confin'd Tuning; and that you have undertook what you underftand not; nor are ever likely to bring to pafs, the way you go to work. And indeed, no one that does underftand Mufick can expect other: For while we muft be one while in the Line with a Note, another while in Space with the fame Note; one while condemn the Monofyllables for Gibberifh, Conjuring, and the learning of them the very drudgery of Mufick; another while command the ufe of them, then eat them; here to fix *Mi* in one of two places only, there in any place; here obliged to the ufe of four Lines only, there to fourteen, or as many as you pleafe; here tied to the ufe of Notes as the moft eafie and intelligible way, thare to the lazy-witted Invention of Tablature; here to exprefs Mufick in the moft familiar words, there to abandon the plain *Englifh* of a great or leffer Third, Fourth, Fifth, *&c.* to imbrace the old Heathen *Greek* Terms, and what not? while I fay we are brav'd from our own fixednefs to thofe pitiful fhilly-fhally's, and altogether infignificant and impertinent pretences; what, Sir, can be expected? Truely nothing that I can any way imagin; except perhaps that thereby we might be made inftrumental to proclame to the World, *That a young Graduate had lately Publifhed Two Books, as exactly agreeing with their Titles as a Pretended Gofpel-Minifter's Sermon in the late Civil Wars did to his Text* (the one being *Fear God, Honour the King*; the other, *an impudent Perfwafion*

swasion to carry on the begun Schism and Rebellion:)
but not to so ill an End, though in all probability
with as much Pride and Contempt. Proportionably
you go on, trifling with the *Harpsichord* and *Lute*,
as if the *One* were previously made for the sole
use of your unbarb'd Jews-Trump, the *Cycle*, and
your Servants B M T ; or the *Other* most elo-
quently Harmonious when untouch'd. For to what
end the first is made a *Phanatick* ; the last, when
used, silent (for so, by a wilful mistake both of
my words and meaning, you have made them) except to keep up the laudable custome of swelling
your Book, and amusing the Reader, I know not.

I must confess, Sir, I have not the Practical Use of
the *Lute*; yet have Composed several things for it; and
from thence am sufficiently convinced, that the way of
Tablature is much easier and properer for that Instru-
ment, and the expression of its excellency, than the
way of Notes ; however I shall not judge, but refer it
to those to whom it properly belongs, *viz. such Lute-
Masters as are qualified in both Capacities.* But as to
the *Harpsichord*, I could smile at your idle Imagination, that a Man must have two Heads for the using two
Staves of Lines, for his two Hands *our Cliff-way* ;
and but one Head for the use of a like two Staves
and two Hands your B M T way, did I not fear
there might be a more than ordinary Mystery in it ;
that is to say, One great Loggerhead with huge
great Saucer-Eyes, like those in the *Turkish* Pa-
radice, to be Champion in the Cause ; and then,
Woe and well-a-day! but I hope better things. In
confidence whereof, I shall boldly affirm, that
among the many ways of Writing for that Instru-
ment,

ment, the most intelligiblest to the Understanding, and easiest to the Eye, is that which divides the *Staves of Lines, and Hands, on the middle Key thereof*; and so gives occasion to ascend and descend (generally) without the least alteration of Cliffs.

[*See the second Example in Pag.* 10.]

This, Sir, your Four Line B M T way, is wholly incapable of; and so incapable of, that in the Example you took from Mr. *Thetcher*, and inserted in your *Essay*, you were forced to acknowledge, by several times chopping and changing *your signifying Letters* in that short Lesson.

To object, some things may notwithstanding be done that way, is short of your Glorious Pretences, where you undertake *All, Easier, and in half the Time*; the contrary whereof is so notoriously known, that, besides the Masters, several Lovers of Novelties, after a little experience, have with scorn laid it aside. Among others, a Person of Honour, Educated in a School near this City, had your *Essay* presented her piping hot, with such Commendation as the Presenter thought it really deserved; the Lady, with as much thankfulness received it, thinking every Minute a Day till the presence and assistance of her Master might make her happy in the injoyment of this new invented Benefit. The Hour came, and to work they went; but, *O the fickle state of Lovers!* e're many days was expired, the heat was so abated, that there was not Charity enough left to keep it out o'th' fire, had not the Masters earnest intreaty preserv'd it from that cruel Death: but all in vain! for the thing being heartless, after a short time, con-

confum'd by that lingring Difeafe which Squire *Ralpho* long before Prophecied would be the end on't ; and fo farewel it ; but not, Sir, to your *Vindication* of it : For there you promife fuch Advantages, as the World was ignorant of before; there, the Reafons of what it Acted by ; and there, that All Compofitions fhould with Eafe be Tranfpofed from one Key to another, &c. Very prety ! if a Man would believe it. Sir, the Advantages you fo perpetually boaft of, are already fufficiently manifefted and known to be Miftakes, onely to abufe the Mafters and delude the Ignorant ; and confequently need no more taking notice of : Your affuring the Dr. of the *now* eafinefs of tranfpofing Compofitions from one Key to another, is a thing fo frequent, that no one is efteem'd a Mafter who cannot do it *Proper*; and he the contrary, that does it no better than you have done your *Aurelia* in in your *Effay*. But, that Men fhould Act and Teach Rationally, and not underftand the Reafon of their fo Acting and Teaching, till you peep'd into the World ; is to make them Beafts, and too too fubtle for any but your felf to unriddle, who have ftock enough to fay any thing.

For my own part, Sir, I never pretended to more of the Mathematicks than what was practicable in Mufick, and that I have fo evidently demonftrated (if you can but give credit to your felf) that I ftand amazed at the confidence of Contradicting no one till now, ever being fo mad, after he had feen a Man do a thing, to teach him how he fhould do it ; yet this is our Cafe ; and this no Perfon can be ignorant of, that is capable of apprehending,
                                                        that

that all Creatures that have Ears are apprehenfive of Sounds, but not of diftinguifhing them; thofe, whofe Ears Nature hath prepared for Practical Mufick, by dividing and fub-dividing a String (for Example) come to experience their difference and diftances; and from thence, by comparing them, to Tones, which (the Ear having diftinguifhed into Confonants and Diffonants) they Arithmetically divide to the greateft quantity Practicable (*viz.* 32.) and thence, by Harmonical Proportion of whole, half, and quarter Tones (altogether fufficient for ufe) advance to That we call *Compofition*, the Mother of all Vocal and Inftrumental Mufick. More of the Mathematicks than this, Sir, (excepting what belongs to the Mechanical Part thereof for the Making Inftruments) fignifies nothing to us; *This*, and not the poring after idle and unpracticable Notions, being that which the Schools defervedly honour with the Degrees of *Batchelor* and *Doctor*, above or equal to all other Sciences. The reft therefore if you pleafe (for you are infinitely free) you may beftow on your unprofitable Speculators; who, fo long as they can think of lengthening a *String*, or adding to *Number*, will never want imployment. This I mention, not in the leaft to contradict thofe Honourable and Excellent Perfons, whofe very Recreations, by their diving into the Bowels of Nature for the Improvement of Art, prove daily advantagious to the World; or to prove that Mufick has got the whip-hand of her Sifter Sciences, and already arrived to the utmoft of Practical Excellency; and fo needs none; but to fhow, that after all your Hectorifh Bravadoes,

you

you have moſt manfully, like your ſelf, quitted the Field of *Practical Muſick*, and run for ſhelter to the *Nature and Cauſes of Sounds*, which properly belongs to Philoſophy, and which you, in confidence perhaps that all Men would greedily ſwallow your imaginary Gudgeon the *Eſſay*, particularly waved in the laſt Page thereof.

And now, Sir, I might with very much reaſon finiſh my Letter; but leaſt many of your admiring Readers may be ignorant of the Subject you undertook to write on, it will not be amiſs I think to give them an Example or two within their own Spheres, of the wild Conſequences you draw from the plain Words in my *Obſervations*; as alſo, to make a particular inſpection into ſome few (amongſt many) of thoſe obliging Favours, you, and your *Goodman*, *Mr. Sr. Min Heer*, *Monſieur*, *Senior Don*, *Dominus ſine Nomine de Norwich* (that Grand Maſter of Grammatical Criticiſm and Cocoriſm) have ſo graciouſly Complemented me with, and ſo conclude.

Where, in my *Obſervations*, I give an account of the timely check I took, when I thought my ſelf to be more than ordinarily knowing (a fault Youth is too ſubject to) you infer *All young Men muſt be Fools.*

When I inſtance the continued Ignorance of the Bear-Garden-Uſher at the end of his Annual Profeſſion, you come out with your, *Ergo, I turn all thoſe venerable Anceſtors into Great Bears.*

When I wonder, that throughout your whole Diſcourſe of Muſicks Advantages over other Recreations, yon mention nothing of the Divine Uſe
thereof,

thereof, notwithſtanding the many Commands and Examples recounted in Holy Writ to that purpoſe, you roundly conclude, *I am ignorant that God is a Scripture-Name.*

When I prove the *Old Scale* to be the moſt certain and eaſieſt way, yet propoſed, for the attainment of Muſick, by the regular ballancing the extreme Parts thereof with removing the *C* Cliff, and the *impertinency* of yours, you cry out, *I'd build a Ladder to reach the Triple Tree of Preferment.*

When I inſert a Phyſicians probable ℞ for the Explanation of the ſuper-abundant Excellencies of your B M T, you infer, *I deter all that underſtand or profeſs Phyſick from the Study of Muſick.*

Theſe, and the like Patterns, your Northern Hector has been exactly careful to conclude by; for from the Exceptions I have made in ſome of my Writings againſt the ill performance of ſome, and needleſs Mathematical impoſitions of others, he ſtoutly avers, *I am the only Confounder of all Muſick;* though almoſt in the ſame Breath, he commends me for my Ability in that Art, and ſeriouſly perſwades me to continue my Studies therein. Which I'le aſſure you, Sir, I take for no ſmall Favour, ſeeing that, by his Exception againſt *Mood, Time,* and *Prolation,* without which, no Muſick ever was or can be made, he bountifully manifeſts his wilful or real ignorance of the Subject he pretends to vindicate.

But *Trim Tram,* 'tis all could be expected; the whole buſineſs being as it ſeems, rather to write, than what, or how? And truely, Sir, had I affected

B   ſuch

fuch kind of Fooling (to fpeak no worfe on't) I might with as much fhew of reafon conclude thus from your Difcourfe and manner of Writing :

Guido *lived in an ignorant Age* ,
But T. S. *ftands on* Guido's *Shoulders :*
Ergo, *Thofe Venerable Anceftors*
T. S. *has ftudied are Great Bears.*

And in all probability , might have given the World as much fatisfaction in that profound way of Arguing, as either of you.

But, Sir, you are not contented to let me efcape thus ; my *Heart* as well as *Opinion* you diffect, and there make fuch a difcovery of Venome, if the *unblemifhed Fame and facred Credit* your Epiftoler gives you, prove true; that I fhould wonder how I lived, did not Experience give a better account of my *Vitals.*

The firft *Viper* you meet with , is *Malice,* which doubtlefs is a Grand Imp of Iniquity wherever found ; but, Sir, that a bare oppofing an Opinion concerning Practice, fhould be that *Beaft,* is a thing no ingenious Man can imagin ; and for your pretty Perfon, I do affure you, I never faw any thing that could beget more than pity towards it , in pretending to fo much Learning, and having fo little Civility.

The fecond, is *Lying* ; wherein, bating Childifh Excufes, and artificial Stories to pafs the time with now and then, I never knew my felf *formally* guilty of; but truly, Sir, were the *Saddle* fet on the right Horfe, an Acquaintance of mine would have a great Burthen ; for he cannot be content to belye his Neighbors, but himfelf too. Who,
but

but he, Sir, do you think would have affirmed, *That the Observer would have approv'd the Essay* (and render'd himself a Knave to Posterity) *for a good Fish-Dinner souc'd in Wine?* Who, but he, *would protest that he never required or used more than one ascititious Line over or under the five*, when in the Plate of his Diagram he adds another, and both contrary to his first Principle, for *Four Lines only?* Who, but he, *that the Observer was forced to quit the Places of his Obligations at* Hackney *for his ill behaviour?* (the contrary whereof will with Truth and Modesty, be testified by all the Persons, from the Mistresses to the Servants, during his Converse there.) And who, but he, or *Old Nick* for him, *That those excellent Young men of His Majesties Chappel, did many of them perfectly understand the Rudiments of Musick before His Majesties happy Return?* The contrary being so evident, that for above a Year after the Opening of His Majesties Chappel, the Orderers of the Musick there, were necessitated to supply the superiour Parts of their Musick with *Cornets* and *Mens feigned Voices*, there being not one Lad, for all that time, capable of Singing his Part readily.

Prophaneness and *Immodesty* advance next: Concerning which, I have not as yet attain'd to that Pharisaical Sanctity (or rather Hypocrisie) to justifie every Word or Action of my Life, I am more sensible of the Defects of Humane Nature, and hope, shall be more and more, till my happy Change come. But to write prophanely, is a thing I ever abhorr'd, and in confidence I never was guilty of that Sin, I challenge you, and your Brother Trum-

peter,

peter, to produce one Word that any rational Man shall judge to be so. And for Immodesty, 'tis pleasant to see, how, after you, and your angry Admirer's detesting that *Paw* ℞ in my *Observation*, and crying out against it, *'tis such stuff as a Man would not touch with a pair of Tongs* (as if you were of that *Sect* who pretend to have found an Art for Propagating Mankind without Females) that neither of you can keep it out of your Mouths, you are so in love with it : A cunning way to correct Vice, doubtless ! and not much unlike those Brethren of iniquity, *who could quickly espy a Mote in their Brothers Eye , but not take the least notice of the Beam in their own*, planting themselves into the *Row* of the Just , with this misapplied *Salvo, To the clean all things are clean*. This is Prophaneness too, Sir, is it ? If it be, 'tis only to those whose straight-laced Consciences will permit them *to strain at a Gnat, and swallow a Camel* ; not to those who endeavour to walk by that great Law of *Doing as they would be done to*. And so farewel *Prophaneness* , and your never to be honoured *Apocryphal Beast*.

Ignorance succeeds ; which I heartily acknowledge my self to be stored sufficiently with, especially in the *Scholastick way of Railing* , wherein you, and your *Honourable Hand-man* are excellent : But, that after the spending most part of my Studies in Composing *Divine Hymns* and *Psalms* , both in *Latin* and *English*, taken out of the *Holy Scripture*, either immediately as they lie , or collected as occasion requir'd, *to remain ignorant that* God *is a Scripture-Name* ; this, Sir, is a Favour above all

Favours,

Favours, and which through *my sides* darts at all the Lay Catholicks in the World, but I'le leave them to anſwer for themſelves. The reaſon of this Charge was, becauſe I ſaid, *you mention'd not a word of the Divine Uſe of Muſick in your Eſſay*; which under favour, Sir, I muſt ſay, and ſay again; for, for you to urge that God was the Author of it, is ſhort of the purpoſe, *he being the Author of every good and perfect Gift*, whether uſed in or out of his *Divine Service*; or, to ſay that 'twas uſed as a means to allay *Saul's* Anger; for the care of his Courtiers, whether Prieſts, Prophets, or others, were to find a *Cunning Harper* to quiet him, not to procure an Act of Devotion in him; no more than what is done in the Caſe of one bitten by a *Tarantula*.

But the *Caſe* is thus: That as you begun your Book *with the Advantages of Muſick above other Recreations*; ſo, after you had ſpun out your Diſcourſe, and *waved* even Philoſophy to mix with it, which you know, Sir, is but the Hand-maid to Divinity and Divine Worſhip; you conclude it, without ſo much as taking notice of either, thus: *But this is ſo far from our Practical Propoſal, that it may ſuffice to have given theſe hints, and ſo withdraw, leſt while I plead for Muſick, as a noble and lawful Divertiſement, it ſhould be found guilty of encroaching upon thoſe more ſerious Studies, to which it is to be only a Recreation.*

By what hath hitherto been ſaid, I hope, Sir, the indifferent Reader will be ſatisfied, that the *Malicious, Lying, Ignorant, Immodeſt, Prophane* Parts of your Charge againſt me, are not on my

ſide,

fide ; but have with as much Modesty as their nature would permit, return'd from whence they
came ; though from your felf, nothing is to be expected, being you have long fince declared your
refolution, never to be convinced. There remains
now, one only little Favour, which you have been
pleafed to beftow upon my *Perfon*, that *Mind* and
Body might be equally Habited, which is, your
rendering me Squint-Eyed ; and truly, Sir, 'tis of
the fame Tincture with the former.

Had I been *Purblind, Copper-Nos'd, Sparrow-
Mouth'd, Goggle-Ey'd, Hunch Back'd*, or the
like, (Ornaments which the beft of my Anta-
gonifts are adorn'd with) what work would there
have been with me ? but, thanks be to Heaven,
Nature has done her part, and fo prevented your
farther Liberality on this poor Body of mine, and
confequently faved me the Labour of following your
Tract into fuch unfrequented Paths, as you have
been forc'd to run through, from the Subject you
firft undertook, *to Make a Book*, that whofoever
fhall put himfelf to the trouble of a ferious perufal
of, will not at all wonder, that Books are Publifhed *of the Contempt of the Clergy*, when fuch as
you, who have undertaken the Cure of Souls,
fhould fpend that Precious Time, in vilifying and
detracting thofe Perfons, *especially Muficians*, who
have been fo favourable in their frank Inftructions
and Affiftances to your felf ; the due reward whereof in many grave Mens Opinion, being rather a
P— than a P—

And fo, Sir, with the like Advice you were
pleafed to give me, from the good Example of
Mr.

Mr. *Chr. Simpson* (referring the Piquant Part of your Book to the Man in Buff) I take my leave, remaining,

Sir,

Your very thankful Servant,

From my Lodgings in the Strand, July 24, 1672.

M. L.

Duellum Musicum :

OR THE

MUSICAL
DUEL.

Hat a murrain is the matter here? that a Man cannot give his Friend half a dozen Lines, but he muft be fo hufft and bufft, and rebufft, and fnufft and pufft at, by a half-witted *Trinitonian?* A *Univerſitie Chicken* that *peep-peeps* about the Town ftill, with his Shell upon his Head. What ftrange *Cimmerian* darknefs have we liv'd in hitherto, that we muft be beholding to this upftart *Ignis Fatuus* to light us into the right Paths of Mufick? What a difmal obfcurity does this quick-fighted *Argos* find our *Noble Science* wrapt in, that he fo ob-
fequioufly

sequiously stands at the corner of every
Street, crying out to the stumbling Musitians, *Will ye have a Link, sir ?* A prety
young confident *Essayer*, that will be per-
ching up to the Title of a Reformer, before he can prattle sense. Such another
kind of *Innovator* was *Jack Straw*, who
would fain be pulling down, before he
knew what to set up in the place. Or, as
if *Taylor*, the *Waterman*, should have endeavour'd a Reformation in Poetry, by
debasing *Spencer*, and crying up his own
extravagant Shreds of Nonsense. What a
long Maggot did possess that young Skull
of his, when he thought by such Absurdities, to begin a Correction of Musick.
For what is that Ricketty *Embryo* of his
kickshaw Brain, ycleped B M T, but as
if he intended to set up another *Perkin
Warbeck*, to disinherit the lawful Issue of
one of the most Noble Sciences in the
World.

Does this Fidling Potentate intend to
maintain an Army of *Amanuenses*, to tran-
scribe the Legions of Musical Volumes,
and Scores already either in Writing or in
Print? Or, is it his own Fanatick Attempt
(for it deserves not the appellation of Design)

fign) to plunge the World into an Abyſs of Ignorance, and to confine our Knowledge within the narrow *Circle* of his own *Stupid Circulation?* Suppoſe B M T were ſent with a Sett of Mottetts to the Pope; what could the poor things expect, but the ſevere puniſhment of the *Inquiſition*, or the ſame hard Fate of direful *Excommunication* which *Virgilius* had for aſſerting the *Antipodes*, and there is as much reaſon for it, for the one ſets Men, the other Muſick on her Head. Whence ſome do conjecture, that however this modeſt Batchelor do inveigh ſo much againſt *Baudy*, yet that he has no unkindneſs for a quaint *Apparition*. Would ever any Man elſe have ſet Muſick in ſuch a ſtrange poſture with her Heels upwards? And thus ſtanding on her Head, ſhe muſt be expos'd not only to Men, but to Boys; who muſt be now forc'd to begin from the Baſe to learn their way to the Treble. Oh the ſtrange, and yet remaining Effects of the Year 666! It has bred another kind of a *Copernicus* with a *Circulating Octave*, that would have *Muſick* ſpin like a Caſting-Top, becauſe his own Childiſh Brains are ſtill taken with the ſport.

But

But I shall leave that Idol of *Bell* and the *Dragon*, to be altogether demolish'd by a Person, whom the *Vindicator* seems very much to slight, even Mr. *J. Playford* himself, whom I think an Antagonist deep enough in all Conscience for such a Master of Arts as he is: And that notwithstanding the *Vindicator* twits him with writing himself *Philo-Musicæ* (a Fault no Scholar would have taken notice of from such a Person) yet I cannot find, but that by his own sedulity he hath attained to more knowledge in Musick than ever the *Vindicator* is like to do; and that he has done more for the *Advancement of Musick* than ever that Bauble the *Essay* is like to produce. Such Novelties and Paper Projects as these, unless the Person be of a subtle Ingenuity, his Arguments very weighty, and the Use and Profit of the Invention be very apparent, are but *Volusi Annales*, meerly *Charta cacata*: And therefore for this bauling *Codrus*, I am resolv'd to have a fling at his Jacket, though I lose by the bargain. As for the *Observer*, because I dare not presume, though the rash *Essayer* does, to be so Excellent in Musick as he is, I shall therefore leave him to his own Affair: Only

Only as the *Vindicator* has his touches at me by the by; so I am resolv'd to have my touches at him by the by.

In the first place I observe, He has been very kind to his Pamphlet, to commend it into the Hands of a Person who is reported to be very little affected with the Subject, either desiring his three *dumb Brats* might be taught to speak, or else reprieving his *Infant Cogitations* from the Tragical Candle, or more dishonourable death of the Close-stool; which else must have been their certain Fate, had they fall'n into the Hands of any other Man, who (to use the Language of his own Sect) had understood the *empty Nothingness* thereof.

Pag. 2. He wonders *He should receive so little respect*, since he *professes himself to be a Graduate of one of the most Noble Universities in the World.* And truly I wonder how he durst profess himself one of the number. Surely he was either a very great Truant, or else of a very unperforable Pericranium; for he shews but a slender sign of his University-Education: Where he seems to have spent his time rather in the more laudable Exercises of Trap and Cricket,

Cricket, than in any found Reading; having only leifure to adorn, and all to bedeck his furreptitious Master-of-Art-fhip with the flatulent, droffie, and unwholfome part of Mock-Learning. So that his *Alma Mater* has the leaft reafon in the World to thank him for his taking notice of her. Much better had it been, fince he would give himfelf the Title of *Mafter of Art*, to have wrote himfelf *ex Ambuhajarum Collegio*; a thing we fhould have much fooner believ'd, than his being of *Trinity College*.

He is very angry to be compar'd to the *Gentleman Ufher of the Bears*, which he out of his great Experience in reading *Venerable Anceftors*, terms the *Metamorphofis* of himfelf into a *Jackanapes*. For my part, I confefs, I can pick out no fuch Meaning out of the Words; however 'tis fitting the Gentleman fhould have the Liberty of his own Interpretation, fince no body knows what fhape beft becomes him, better than himfelf.

He goes on, *And all thofe Venerable Anceftors we read*— Pray, good Sir, let me entreat you to leave out the *We* : You read *Venerable Anceftors* ! — *ridete mortales* —

Men

Men that read *Venerable Ancestors*, never want what is common to all Mortals, only some few *Masters of Art*, the thing call'd *Common Sense*; and when they take an Author to pieces to answer him, never mistake the plain and palpable Meaning of the Words. I am not so fond, to think the *Observer* so unwary, to compare such a dwindling *Vindicator* to *David*, in that sense which he assumes to himself, that is not able to conquer the little *wrigling Magots* he snaps at : Or to liken him to *Hercules*, otherwise than as the Proverb led the *Observer*, to shew, by his silly beginning, what a wise end he was like to make.

He now comes to an open Confession of his Inabilities: though afterwards, out of a most disingenious Repentance, he would fain put it off with an Ironie, by which, he endeavours to insinuate a larger Commendation of himself; but the Plot's discover'd, and, as the Devil would have it, by his own particular self; for he that a little before was aspiring to be a *Goliah*, a *David*, a *Hercules*, now condescends to be *granted* a *Sot*, a *Coxcomb*, nay *any thing*, rather than not have a Name in the World. Truly 'tis pity no body will take the pains,

to

to make him the Subject of another *Moriæ Encomium* : I humbly conceive, it would be no *Paradox*, as the *Former* was. He makes a small attempt to be a kind of an *Oedipus* also, and to put forth a Riddle; talking, *numine Fanatico afflatus*, of *Burlesque upon Poetry*, and *Verse upon Burlesque*: prety words indeed, however he had the good luck to come by 'um; but since they stand there without Rhyme or Reason, we are bound to believe, that he made use of 'um only to shew us his great skill and reading in *Venerable Anceſtors*.

He goes on, with much meekness confeſſing himself to be what indeed he is, a very inconsiderable waſter of clean Paper; rendring himself much more contemptible by that vain and ridiculous ſuperbity, that peeps through the Pillory of his own feigned *Humility*. Truly thoſe notable Expreſſions of *Augur-hole*, and *behind the Wainſcot*, do very well become him : A right worſhipful *Master of Arts*, and of long ſtanding, and a very great Ornament to *one of the most Noble Univerſities in the World*, that has hardly yet forgot his Childiſh Plays of *All Hid*, and *Fools Corner*.

But

But now, *Libera nos Domine*; there is a strange *Hobgoblin* stands in his way, which his foresaid *Humility* seems much to fear, but his foregoing *Pride* seems much to scorn; *A terrible Fellow in Buff*; to encounter whom, he seems to have put a great share of that little wit he has, upon the dry Grindstone of his empty Common place-Book; where after a long search, he finds *Mercury* to be in Conjunction with *Mars*, and therefore gives him the Title of *Epigrammatical Poetaster*. See how this *University Mushrome* begins to swell with the Poyson of his own conceited Imaginations. He that has as little judgment in Poetry, as he has in Musick, and understands an Epigram no more than a wild Inhabitant of *Nova Scotia*, will be nibling at *Characters*, as little to be regarded as his *Ponderous Essay*, or his impertinent *Vindication* that follows.

Nescis, crede mihi, quid sint Epigrammata, Flacce.

It might be expected perhaps the poor Worm should turn again, when trod upon; but 'twas expected withall, that his *Trinity*

C   *Loins,*

Loins of Mutton fhould have infpired his *Genius* with a more keen Fancy , efpecially againft a *Man in Buff* ; for I do not find that the moft piercing of all his Paper-Pellets has made the leaft fign of a razure in any part of the *Buff-Coat* he fo fmartly fhoots at. But ye cannot blame him for making fo ill ufe of his weak Artillery , that appears to be fo fetter'd and entangled in the application of a Story. Gentlemen, 'twas in fhort thus : *Marfyas* was a *Phrygian* , a party-per-pale *half Scholar, half Ignoramus*, who would needs propofe to *Apollo* a Thing call'd an *Effay for the Advancement of Mufick* : *Apollo* laught at it , but becaufe he would not be his own Judge , he chofe many others ; and then returns an *Anfwer*. *Marfyas* replyes, by way of *Vindication*. But the Judges found the *Effay* and the *Vindication* to be fo extraordinary frivolous , that they order'd *Marfyas* to be flead alive for his prefumption. This Story grates upon the Ears of the *Trinity Scholar* (as it behoves every Man to look to his own Flefh) and therefore to allay the fury of a certain Spirit in Buff, which his own Guilt has difcovered, he has provided himfelf, from the Hands of fome *South-wark mark* Sorcerer, as is conjectur'd, of a most powerful *Charm* or *Spell*, consisting of two *Trithemian* Words , *Epigrammatical* and *Poetaster* ; for that you may be sure was his intention, seeing most Charms are commonly composed of insignificant Words. And to make it the stronger , he has found out another piece of Witchcraft, which he calls *Defunct*. A word, which I do assure him the *Man in Buff* never so much as dreamt of ; being nothing but what his quaint cunning only did invent , to raise to himself the superstructure of a paltry University Quibble, and that with so much straining at wit , as easily discovers the costiveness of his Brains. They that will take the pains to read it , may thereby soon find out , what a Great *Master of Art* can do, if he be hard put to't. But had a Man prais'd him, it had been all one , for 'tis not the quality, but the quantity which he grumbles at. For now he seems not so mad that Verses were made upon him , but that there were no more of the same kind ; as if he measur'd the goodness of Lines , by the length of the Vicars Hour-glass , or the tediousness of his own Repetitions. Gentlemen, I am but one , and therefore

let

let me defire you to make a Collection among ye, that this our fecond honeft *Tom Coryat* may not want the full defire of his heart. And fo good Mr. *Sheepskin* the *Man in Buff* moft kindly bids you Farewel.

Thus far the *Exordium*. Now enter *Vindicator in propria perſonâ*, yclad not in *Buff*, but in a colour fomething a kin to it, with a little mixture of *Red*. If you like him not in that ſhape, you may imagin him to be fome Mountebank curvetting upon the Stage with a Remedy for Frenzies, or a ſleepy Potion for Chyrurgeons to uſe while they cut off Gangren'd Limbs ; for the following Pages are fuch Hum-drum, drowſie, heavy, impertinent ſtuff, that a a Man can hardly read 'um over without putting himſelf to all the inconveniences of Opium : 'Tis like *Lethe* or the *Lotos* Tree. And one would ſwear that the Author had either drank the one, or eat of the Fruit of the other, for he preſently falls into a fantaſtical Dream, and ſeems to ſit talking idly to himſelf of a certain A-rithmetical Myſtery of the Beaſt, which he has compendionfly reduc'd from the Numbers 666 to the Number 81. A ſubtle kind of trifle that might perhaps have
troubl'd

troubl'd the Brains of *Napier* or *Broughton*, or fomebody elfe as mad as they, or himfelf, but never to be admitted within the Verge of a fenfible Obfervation. His fuppofition of a Tavern-Invitation, is nothing but meer School-boys prattle, and favours onely of the Folly of a contemptible Scribler.

But now, guilty by his own confeffion of the drowfie *flatnefs* of his foregoing Lines, the Gentleman promifes much Wit, an abundance of Wit, yea even a fuperfluity of Wit; but proves the arrant'ft Cheat in Nature; there not appearing from him from this place to his very *Finis*, fo much as one *Univerfity Punn*, to fave his credit: Only a few undigefted Ironies, ill-contriv'd Reproaches, fcandalous Mifquotations, and pitiful Vaunting of his own mighty Acts, with a *here I have him* and *there I have him*, *I'le pull him down*, and *I'le crufh him*; all which are fo far from Wit, that they only fmell of the Lees and Grounds of the College-Butlers Tappings. They afford not difcourfe fublime enough for a Suburb Coffee-houfe.

He begins with a *Tale* of a *Tale*; but I dare fay, had the *Scare-crow*, which he has

fo

ſo wittily (by long obſervation of the Girls dreſſing their Babies at home) ſtuft *with ſtraw*, and accoutred with an *old hat*, and a *dirty muckinder*, been to make Remarks upon the ſame *Tale*, he would have done it with more ſoul and vigour, and leſs miſtaken the Authors progreſs to *Application*. Which he, like a moſt juſt *Vindicator*, according to his uſual Method, has moſt faithfully and cordially done. Elſe might he have well applied the Story to himſelf, and made an eaſie diſcovery from the *Obſervers Tale*, what a ridiculous thing it is, for a Young-man to be pragmatical beyond the compaſs of his knowledge.

In the Name of *Rabbi Abraham*, what are theſe? *Galtruchius* and *Ariſtoxenus* both Conjured up, and thruſt by Head and Shoulders into a Diſcourſe, no more *ad Rhombum*, than the Quotations they are forc'd to avouch. For I know no body ſo uncivil to him as to deny him his *ſeven Voices*, ſo that he might have preſerv'd both his *Greek* and his *Latin* Breath to have cool'd his Univerſity Porridge. Only by this you are bound to take notice, that he has not been at *Oxford* for nothing, but that either he himſelf can read *Greek*, or ſome body
                                                                    elſe

elſe for him. By the way, Friend, I adviſe you, not to ſpeak evil of *Lycoſthenes*, for I am afraid by theſe *Quotations* pickt out of *Indexes*, that he is one of your beſt Friends.

A ſecond reaſon of this moſt pompous ſhew of his illuſtrious Learning, was perhaps to remind you of his Reading *Venerable Anceſtors:* Elſe would he never have taken upon him ſuch an *Herculean* Toyl of bringing together his mouldy ſcraps of *Greek* and *Latin*, to prove that which no perſon ever contradicted, nor indeed was ever dreamt to be the Subject of the Diſpute: Like the Country Parſon, that being neceſſitated to ſhew all his *Greek* before the Biſhop of the Dioceſs, quoted an Amorous Diſtich out of *Muſæus*, which had been beaten rather into his Buttocks than his Head, to prove the Reſurrection.

In the next place he makes a *Gladiatorlike* Flouriſh : Quoth he, *Come therefore, as* J. Philips *calls thee, come thou* Apollo, *thou Sign of a Sun Tavern.* Pray Gentlemen do me the kindneſs to ſhew me where the Cream and Marrow of this Conceit lies, for a Jeſt I dare not allow it to be ; unleſs it be a Jeſt for ſuch a *Pedler* in *Muſick, fick*, with his Fardle of new-fangled *Gin-gombobs*, to think with an infipid *Nick-Name*, to fully the Skill of a *Perfon* fo much above the reach of his Capacity. Had he produc'd as much Salt, as (if he had petition'd for it) the loweft Form in *Paul's* School could have lent him, he might have made fome progrefs in his Attempt. 'Tis no wonder Men fay the World is turn'd *arfie verfie*, when the *Sign-Poft* fhall prefume to undervalue the *Sign*. But prefently as if the Gentleman had miftaken his Mark, he calls the *Obferver* the Sun's *Rival Luminary*. *Come*, quoth he, *fee the Circuit of thy Rival Luminary, fee the like Circulation of the imitating Blood*. What a heavenly Rapture is the Gentleman now in? How his fond Soul skips and leaps, like a fat Heifer in the plentiful *Elyfian Fields* of *Nonfence?* But whence all this joy? only to behold a *Conundrum* of his own Invention, ftoln out of *Old Butler*, though to difguife the *Theft* he has periwigg'd the prety *Engin* with about half a dozen fmall Lines of his own Trimming. There you find the thing that tickles his his Spleen; B M T riding Triumphant in a Chariot grac'd with one Wheel, while

the

the *Vindicator* like *Biton*, or *Cleobis* draws about his three *Cybele's* to be ador'd in the pig-market, in hopes of some strange remuneration. An excellent *Gimcrack* for the Foot-boys in *Lincolns-Inn-Fields* to throw Dice upon: For to say truth, his pilfer'd Scheme, so admirable in his own Eyes, is but a meer toy, and shews you nothing, but what has been for many Years *lippis & tonsoribus notum.*

Therefore let him e'ne take his *Rota*, and present it to the grave Burghers of the Common-wealth of *Oceana*; for I find it is somewhat of the Nature of the Stork, 'twill hardly live under a Monarchy.

Now heav'ns preserve the three fair Goddesses, B M T, for their *Celestial Auriga* is just about to drive them through a most uncouth *Desart*, where they are like to meet with all the Incumbrances that can put them to the squeek, or stop the merry motion of their *single-wheel'd Chariot*. Here you shall find them jolted by the stump of a *Hexacordon*; there half over-turned by a rude heap of *Pentachordons*; in another place ready to be tumbled down the precipice of a *Tetrachordon*. By and by he whirls through an inchanted Vale of
Fractions

Fractions and *Logarithms*, to deſtroy the poor diſtreſſed *Gamut*, with as much fury, as *Don Quixot* aſſaulted the Wind-mill : And all this ſweat, pains and toyl to as much purpoſe, in reference to the Eſtabliſhment of his new *Whimwham*, as if he had ſet down in place of his *trite* and common *proportions*, the Hiſtory of the Wiſe Men of *Gotam*. Methinks out of the abundance of his learning, and the quaintneſs of his Invention, he might have ſtudied a new way how to avoid thoſe chap-tiring words, with which he amuſes his *Young Beginners*, and have made his *Mother Tongue* beholding to him for teaching her to expreſs in her own Idiom, the Noble Science of *Muſick*, of which ſhe is ſo much the Miſtriſs, and he ſo much the Maſter. That had been an employment far better becoming him, than to ſit ſo amorouſly all day long chucking his three fair Miſtreſſes, B M T, under the Chin. But ſince all this while he hath neither done that, nor any thing elſe for the advancement of his *Eſſay*, we ſhall abandon his frivolous *Arithmetick*, together with his *Corollary*, to the neceſſary uſes of Human Nature. Only one thing we are to take notice of, becauſe he pretends

tends it to be a conceit : 'Tis a pithy one, if you obferve it. For he is perfwaded that the *Sun appear'd lately with a circle about it, in his defence* againft the *Obferver Apollo, its Corrival.* Would you have thought that *Philofophy* could have found out fuch an exquifite fignification of a *Halo.* But this it is to be a man of Invention ; this it is *by the Errancy of the blood to have a great Confluence of Spirits to the brain.* Let any man tell me where there is fuch a tranfcendent Notion in all *Dubartas,* or where-ever *Schoggan* fpake any thing fo ingenioufly ; *Et erit mihi magnus* Apollo.

He is next defired to refolve a fair Queftion ; *To what purpofe are all his Mathematical contrivances, whether they will teach a man to make air, or maintain the point of a* Canon? To which, he with a moft acute gravity, and a wary prudence anfwers , as if a man fhould fay, *There were three Cooks of Colebrook.*—— For as for his defire *to know the nature and reafon of Mufick ;* or his exhortation to *admire the glorious order of its Compofure,* certainly any man that will, may do all that, without the ridiculous *Affiftance* of his *Fiddle-faddle* B M T. This fhort and fweet exhortation, being ended , he he *sinks* again, as he himself confesseth, into the tedious repetitions of his beloved *Essay*; as if he had undertaken to be a Champion rather for the *Cuckow* than the *Nightingale*. And his wonderful drift is to bring his *Dear First-born* into the favour of the World, which he would fain have ro cherish his *malapert Stripling*; and to believe that he writes man, before the poor Child can speak plain. By which he thinks to angle to himself a notable business: For, quoth he to himself, If I could but perswade the World, that all my *Fore-fathers* were *puppies* to *me*; and that there was nothing of *true Musick* upon the face of the Earth, before I came to be Two and Twenty Years of Age; then would all the ignorant race of Mortals be forc'd to come trom the North, and the South, and the East, and the West; yea, from every point of the Compass, to learn *Musick* of *Me*: And I should be the only Teacher under the spreading Canopy of Heav'n. Now that this is the *Advancement of Musick*, which he so craftily designs, is as plain as his pretty picture before his Book, for why? He is come already from *proposing*, to *professing*; and to shew what high things he aims at, he invites

all

all *His Majesties honourable Servants* to go
to School to him at *Hackney,* Famous for the
Seminaries of young Girls; but never famous that ever I heard of before for the
Inftruction of *His Majefties Honourable Servants :* They may take their Bottles and
their Baskets, and go if they pleafe; but
I fear the blemifh he has laid upon them of
wanting the knowledge of the *Nature* and
reafons of Mufick, till furnifh'd from fuch a
Bawble-ftall as his, has quite knock'd out
the brains of his Infant project.   And fo
Gentlemen, you may fafely pafs over to his
32 *p.* without the leaft detriment to your
future knowledge: For I'le fay that for
him and a fig for him, that he is the moft
cautious perfon how he puts his Friends to
the trouble or neceffity of writing much,
that ever I met with.

In his 32 *p.* you may find him fimp'ring to
himfelf, with a *Sardonick* fmile to fee his
publifher, (as he out of his copious ftock of
moft ingenious and fcurrilous Eloquence
terms it) fo *arrogantly* affaulted.   See how
this little fly upon the Coach-wheel, would
vaunt and ftrut if it could !   Good lack a-
day !   what a crime it was to affault his publifher ?   How the poor thing begs and
                                          fcrapes

ſcrapes for applauſe ! as if his deſerts were
ſuch as could keep his publiſher from being
aſſaulted. Alaſs, we underſtood the worth
of his *Publiſher*, without the aſſiſtance of
his lean Commendations : And we hope ſo
well of him, that when he was pleaſed to
countenance ſuch a parcel of Thrums and
Mop-rags, as was the worſhipful *Eſſay*,
'twas only in compliance with *Horace*, a
better Author than ever he will be ; who
tells ye, that ſometimes it is — *Dulce deſi-
pere in loco* — which we are the more apt
to believe, becauſe it is very credibly affirmed that the Gentleman has ſince openly
and candidly diſclaim'd and deſerted the
Vindicator's forlorn cauſe as altogether un-
worty of his Patronage, declaring, he never gave him countenance or Commiſſion
to write ſo many extravagant falſities and
fopperies, or to ſow his ſcandals and abuſes
within the verge of his protection.

His taxing the Obſerver with underſtanding nothing but *Morley, Simpſon,* or *Gree-
tings Inſtructions,* I only mention to compleat the number of his predantick Follies ;
but ſhall leave it to *impartiality* it ſelf, to
proclaim the difference between the *Vindi-
catours* green Extravagancies, and the *Obſervers* Experience. As

As for his fcandalous reproach thrown upon the *Obferver*, as if he were ignorant of *the* Names of *God*, *Jubal*, or *Saul*, as it is a cavil founded upon a fhallow furmife of his own; an unfeemly reflection, without any ground, upon a man's Religion, fo it betrayes him not only to a hard opinion of his Scholarfhip, but of his Gentility, and that he has converft more with Kitts and Petticoats, than with men of Education.

But now the Scene alters, and enter *Vindicator*, like *Sampfon*, between the two *Pillars* of *Dagons Temple*, ready to *pull down the Obferver in his ruin*. Truly for ftrength, I fear *Sampfon* will out-do him; but for going blindly to work, 'tis a Cockpit lay of the Effayers fide.

Hoyday — What's here? More of his Learning? More *Bloffommings* of his *Mafter of Artfhip?* Stop him there. He has robb'd the Univerfity of all her reafon at once; and hid the *Promethean* Theft in an old rotten, dirty, muftie Thing, which as I fuppofe, he intended for a Syllgoifm.

S'life quoth *Keckerman*! What abominable dunce made this? Sacrament! quoth *Burgerfdicius*, In the name of the Lords of *Holland* and *Weft-Freefland*, What's here? Blefs

Bleſs me ! quoth *Ramus*, I vow, quoth he ,
I never ſaw ſuch a griſly, diſmal , horrible
ſpectacle in all the *Pariſian Maſſacre.* And
ſurely thoſe great Logicians might well
wonder : For ſuch a miſhapen, deformed ,
crump ſhoulder'd , Baker-legg'd piece of
Vanity, was never born of a Man's brain.
Twenty Bears in Twenty Years cannot lick
it into form : And to uſe the palmes of his
own hands, and faſting ſpittle for the ſame
purpoſe, would waſt him into an Anatomy.
With what face can he pretend to be a
graduate of one of the moſt Noble Univerſi-
ties in the World , and produce ſuch *a what*
ſhall I call it , for a Syllogiſm. The Gentleman indeed had need cry *p.* 59, *hold* his
ſides, while he mocks at other folks , that
has ſo ridiculouſly hamper'd his own reputation, in the ſnare of ſuch a counterfeit
piece of St. *Martins* Ware. Who can believe the *Eſſayer* knows *fingers from toes ,*
as he thinks he does, *p.* 59. that can no better diſtinguiſh between a *Syllogiſm* and a
Chimæra , or between *Logick* and *Canting.*
He would do well to carry it to *Bartholo-*
mew Fair, 'twould be as pretty a ſight to
a Scholar as the *Tall Woman,* or an *African*
Monſter. Now that you may behold this
                                                    Sign

Sign of the Elephant and Caftle, turn to his 41 *p.* where you fhall find the *Pageant* dreft up in all its *Pontificalibus.*

That way which requires an abfurdity five times over is much more to be exploded than that which requires it but once.

But the Obfervers Old way does require the fame (condemning) abfurdity five times, which the Effayers New one requires but once.

Therefore the Obfervers Old way is much more to be exploded than the Effayers New one.

My firft Objection againft this Sillogifm (fhame faw the lugs of our Mafter of Art) is, that though it confift of *Englifh* words, yet that it is neither true fenfe, nor true *Englifh:* A fad ftory, that a Mafter of Art cannot make *Englifh* of *Englifh.* *That way which requires an abfurdity five times over,* and *that way which requires it but once.* Did ever any Mafter of Art fo forget himfelf, as to grant that any Art or Science can *require an Abfurdity?* For,

Dato uno Abfurdo fequuntur Mille.

Behold here a *Trinity* Fly entangled in
D　　　　　　　the

the Cobwebs of his own Learning. Is this
the bragging *Puller down* and *Crusher* that
Rodomontado'd fo but juft now? View
where the mighty *Sampson* lies with the
locks of his own ambitious ftrength quite
cutt off by his own *Dalilahs* B M T. And
now Mafter of Art, have a care, have a
care, for the *Philiftines* are upon thee.
The Common Law of Senfe and Reafon
which thou haft broken, Profecutes thee.
Thomas Salmon, M. A. of *Trin. Coll. Oxon,*
hold up thy Hand; for thou ftandeft en-
dited for the felonious murder of a Sillogifm, contrary to the Statutes of Logick
in that cafe made and provided; and more
than that, for counterfeiting the Kings *English,* and the Stamp of Soveraign Reafon;
of all which thy Country hath found thee
guilty : And now what haft thou to fay
why Sentence fhould not pafs againft thee
according to Law? March to the Place of
Execution; and fo the Lord have mercy
on thee, for a Poor Scholar.

Having objected againft the *English*; I
am in the next place to condemn the *form*
of the *Sillogifm*; For this is a certain Rule,

Conclufio non differt a queftione.

But

But his *Major* and *Conclusion* are so far
from agreeing, that the Conclusion which
ought to be a part of the Argument, quite
varies from it.   His Major is ,

*That way which requires an absurdity five
times over, is much more to be exploded then
that which requires is but once.*

His inference is ,

*Therefore the Observers old way is much
more to be exploded than the Essayers New
one.*

Let them that are dim-sighted put on
their Spectacles, and try if they can find
the *Essayers New* one in the *Major* ; which
ought, as he intended his Sillogism, to have
been the extream term of his first Propo-
sition ; which being left out in the Major,
dashes his whole Sillogism in pieces against
the known Maxim of Logick.

*Quòd non debet esse plus aut minus in con-
clusione, quam fuit in premissis.*

In the next place, there ought not in a
Sillogism to be more than *three Terms*. But
in the *Medium* of this Sillogism you shall
find a *fourth Term* by the name of the *Same
Condemning* shoulder'd in ; to what pur-
D 2   pose

pofe the Lord of *Glocefter* knows. It being a thing quite contrary to another Logical Rule,

Omne medium debet effe unicum, quod enim unit, id ipfum debet effe unicum.

Since then, neither by his falfe *Englifh*, nor by his falfe and Illiterate Sillogifm he hath prov'd the Obfervers Old way to have any *abfurdity* at all ; at his requeft , we will freely grant him that *One abfurdity* which he requires, with all appurtenances thereto belonging ; which, (if he have not found out as New and ftrange an Effay in Logick , as he has in Mufick,) he will find to be a great many. And then behold this *Coloffus* of an Argumentator , how ridiculous muft his fall appear , to thofe that fee his maffie Heels tripp'd up by his own *Condefcention* and *Confeffion.* For ,

That way which has one Abfurdity , has a thoufand Abfurdities.

The Effayers New way has one Abfurdity.

Ergo

The Effayers New way has a thoufand Abfurdities. From whence ,

That way which has a thoufand Abfurdities is utterly to be exploded. The

The Essayers New way has a thousand Absurdities.

Therefore the Essayers New way is utterly to be exploded.

On the other side.

That way which has no Absurdity, is to be allowed.

But the Observers Old way has no Absurdity,

Therefore the Observers Old way is to be allowed.

Surely just such a Master of Art was that Cook in *Rome*, upon whom the following *Epitaph* was made, and which may in time with a little alteration serve to immortalize the memory of our *Hackney Logician.*

Hic jacet Jodocus
Qui fuit Romæ *Cocus,*
In Artibus Magister ,
Qui Argumentavit vel bis ter ,
Semel in Celarent *,*
Ut omnes admirarent
Bis in Frisesmorum
Requiescat in Secula Seculorum.

D 3   And

And thus much as concerning a thing call'd a Sillogifm, the *Author* of which, being a certain young man, I advife to take the *Obfervers Horn-book*, and his *Accidence*, and two pieces of Bread and Butter clapp'd together, and get him to School again, and to leave off his Fooling with *Effayes* and *Vindications*, and diving into Arguments, till he have got more Wit and more Learning.

But becaufe the Sillogifm will not take, he is refolv'd to be-lye the *Obferver*; telling ye an idle ftory, that the *Obferver* makes the Sillable *Vt* to *force the Tongue againfl the Roof of the Mouth*. This is altogether falfe: He tells ye indeed, that there are Confonants which will do it, as moft certainly there are; but afcribes no fuch efficacy to that particular *Sillable*, as he with his ufual gift of miftaking, endevours to demonftrate. And therefore his fuppofition that the *Obfervers Tongue hung the wrong way*, was but an effect of the wrong hanging of his own giddy Brains.

But this is common: Even in the next page, behold another piece of his wonted mif-quotation. The Obferver cries out, *O Reformation! how amiable art thou in the Noftrils*

Nostrils of them that cannot see ! Was it ever heard, felt, or understood, that the Toning of the Voice must take its rise from a Semi-tone, &c. This the *Vindicator* calls a resolution in the *Observer to be for the future guided by his seeing, feeling, and understanding No-strils,* and terms it *a most excellent expression to shew* a further *advancement of his Learning.* A meaning he could never have pick'd out of the words, had not some *Jacob Behmen* enlightened his Pericranium, as indeed 'tis very fit that one *Heretick* should help *another.* But 'tis a strange thing, that he that so much scorns the *Horn-book,* should want a fescue for his own understanding. Is it not a miracle, that a *Vindicator* should so grope in the dark, and blunder through his adversaries text, that carries such a spiritual Lanthorn about him, besides the *Flambeaus* of his own Wit and Memory.

But so it is, that now again because he cannot Answer the Question proposed, (as no body did ever expect he should,) that therefore he gives his old preceptor *Misquotation* a Letter of Attorney to speak for him. Truly, my dear Friend, three false Quotations in less than two Pages, are

D 4   not

not so commendable a virtue as you may imagin. What will the World think of your Book, cramm'd with so many imperfect and insipid untruths? A most special *Vindicator*, who because he cannot answer Objections propos'd, will raise other stupid ones of his own, which he thinks himself to have a more facil way of confuting. For whereas the Observer thought it strange, that the *Toning of the Voice should take its rise from a Semi-tone*. He taxes the Observer of accusing him for beginning to learn *the Monosyllables from a Hemi tone*. To which the *Vindicator* answers, *p.* 54, That those Sillables are not *learnt for any airy pleasantness in themselves, but as rudiments to distinguish Notes and half Notes*, &c. Gentlemen you hear his acute and pertinent reply, set off with a ridiculous *Though I have often told him*.

What a *Magnificent Bubble* is this, to talk of *telling* and *answering*, and at the same time to betray such a sottish dotage, as not to know what a true answer is. The thing is so plain, that 'twould be a *Vindicators* folly to insist further on it.

The conceit of having so exquisitely answer'd that Objection, has set him a crow-
ing

ing moft violently upon his own dung hill.
His imagination is highly tickl'd with the
Obfervers telling him that *Miftrefs* Mi *is
rambled out of her Apartment and turn'd
Quean.* But quoth he, *Let her ramble into
all the Apartiments about the Town, fhe fhall
never want a gentleman Ufher, as long as he
is able to man her.* And of this, he is as
fure as that *four two pences make two groats.*
How pleafant the Gentleman is, now he has
got an oportunity to fancy himfelf in *Lute-
ners-Lane* ; for you may guefs at his haunts,
by his fingle Money. You fee, as early day as
it is, how expert he is : And would you have
thought fuch a modeft young man had been
creeping into the Houfes of Iniquity already ? But the Devil oft-times carries
youth to thofe places, out of his great zeal
to make them deteft their Vices. Come,
come, ne're blufh for't : As good abroad
as at home ; For if *Miftrifs Mi* be a Quean,
fhe's one of his own making ; (perhaps
not the firft has been made at a Boarding-
School ,) and fo the Gentleman-Ufher
returns back to his Bed-Chamber , whole-
fomely to advife him, to look well to the
Calves of his own Leggs, and not to be fo
vainly merry with his fmutty and ungentle
reflections

flections upon other mens Conversations.

He tells ye, *he honours Mr. Simpson*, and yet some Pages before, looks upon him so much beneath his *great reading*, that he only thinks him a Companion for the *Observers mean Capacity*. The best on't is, we look upon him as a *real Exception* to all true *Maxims*. For if *honour* were in *honorante*, while he is the bestower, sad were our Condition. But there is no such thing in him, or that can come from him ; it is rather a blemish, than a praise, to be well spoken of by him ; and therefore let him honour e'ne who he pleases.

He proceeds to a great Astonishment at the *Observers resentment, against any propagating the knowledge of Musick*, thereby *thinking* to raise to himself a vain ostentation of his own endeavours. He means doubtless, the famous *Essay :* A worshipful *Advancement of Musick* indeed, which the most ingenious Author durst not trust into the World, without the strong recommendation, and most notable blessing of a Publishers Preface. For which courtisie of helping a lame dog, *Ferunt & aiunt*, that some body or other had paid him in *pecuniis numeratis* four Pound ten Shillings,
which

which render'd that some-body a wise man,
and the Counterfeit Essayer a meer Musical
Cully : And shews you how little Wit or
Memory he had , to tax the Observer for
being Mr. *Playfords hireling.* Alas! had
the Gentleman found there had been any
reputation to have been gotten by the
Essay , He would soon have wrench'd it
out of the *Vindicators* feeble hands, and
assum'd it to himself.

And therefore I would have this idle
contemner of the *Observer*, forbear those
Hackney-windy-Bottle - Ale - expressions *of
my Essay, my way, my Octaves, my Circulation.*
'Twere a modesty more becoming him ,
than the folly of an impertinent *Vindicator*,
and more worth his while, for the fame he
will get by his works. But amongst the
rest of his *My's*, What think you of *My
Stationer?* By my troth , he is well hope
up with an *Author.* I pity the poor man's
case, for in a short time the City will find
him out, and then he must either fine or
hold.

In his 70. *p.* he prosecutes the Observer
for *spoiling his Marriage*, as he pretends,
for declaring him to have a *rubical Complexion.* What a strange *Map of Modesty*
this

this is, to be dafh'd out of Countenance by his own Face? No, No, my dear Friend, 'tis not the Colour will injure you ; but you are fo bafhful, fo modeft , fo nice, fo ftartled at the very found of a baudy word, that it makes the Women believe you have only a little heat in your Face, and none no where elfe. Otherwife a Mafculine complexion would rather promote , than difappoint your *Conjugal attempts.* Nay, I dare affirm , (if it be not as I fay) that the Ladies are fo mild , fo courteous, fo meek , fo endearing , fo obliging , fo tender-hearted , and merciful , that they will never reject a young mans fuit for a pimple upon his Nofe ; nor confent to that wicked intention of the Obferver ; or rather , that wilful miftake of his, of throwing duft in a Squires Face, where he fhould have daub'd his *Pommatum.* Bnt whence comes this red Face? not by Drinking , nor Smoaking. But as Dr. *Lower* learnedly tells ye, Ladies ; *lib. de Sanguine,* a Book which ye have all read, *by the errancy of the Blood ,* which caufes *a great confluence of Spirits to the Brains.* A reafon well urg'd to underftanding Widows and Maids, but not to Illiterate men.

For

For how can this be apply'd to a perfon that
has neither *Brains* nor *Spirits*? 'Tis you,
therefore, (Ladies) that are guilty, and not
the *Obferver*. 'Tis you that have kindled
thofe fires in his Breaft, that have fo fadly
fcorch'd his Countenance ; Difdain not
therefore *your own Martyr*. What though
you have tann'd his Face with the flaming
beams of your Beauty ; yet is his Mind as
white as Snow , and his Thoughts as pure
as *Lambs-Conduit*-Water. For furely no
Pharifee did ever pretend to more Piety
and Virtue, than he affumes to himfelf on
every flight occafion. *Nihil eft te Sanctius
uno* — Nay, this very rednefs of his Complexion forfooth, muft be the Gentleman-
Ufher to his Godly life. He'l make ye
believe fhortly, that his Nofe is the Sun-
fhine of the Gofpel. But all is not gold
that glifters ; for methinks, with a little
crum of Riboldry, as he terms it , in the
Obfervers Anfwer , (fuch as has been ever
allowed in Satyrical replies) I thought
at firft the modeft maidenly Gentleman
would have fall'n into a Fit of the Mother ;
but when I found him chomping and chaw-
ing it fo often in his Vindication , it was
apparent then, that 'twas not Anger which
had

had overcome him ; but the fweetnefs, and
Honey-combnefs of the expreffion , that
had fo ravifh'd his pallate, fo that he could
even have fwallow'd it.   He does fo
tongue it, and lick it, as if 'twere his dear
Concubine B M T.   So often and need-
lefsly repeated, as if he took occafion to
fcold at the *Obferver* , only that he might
have an oppotunity to dandle the delicious
fucket upon the tip of his lafcivious In-
ftrument of tafting.

He endeavours now of his great grati-
tude , to the Obferver, to fhew you , that
he has not been only at the Univerfity, but
at School too , though where with moft
advantage to his Learning, will puzzle a
good Cafuift to judge.   However, in Rob-
bing *Peter* to pay *Paul,* he has made a hard
fhift to tranfcribe a certain Epigram out of
Val. Martial, as he calls him ; a way of citing
Martial that I never knew a Scholar much
guilty of ; but perhaps he took *Val* for *Mar-
tials* Chriften name, and then I cannot blame
him for ufing that cunning mark of di-
ftinction.   But what has *Martial* to do with
the *Obferver ?* why, nothing that I know
of ; but only to tell ye , that the Obferver
wears a Peruque as many other men do ,
                              and

and that he has made ufe of a youthful expreffion, to put a deferved mockery upon
the Harlotry *Dalilah's*, of fuch a young
Pragmaticus. Who, if he had fo pleas'd,
might have obferv'd, that the very Author
whom he cites, makes ufe of far more ri-
baldry (as he calls it) when he meets with
fuch an Impertinent, as the *Effayer*, and
thinks it convenient to have his guils well
rubb'd with his Satyrick Salt. For example, being to reprehend the folly of fome
trifling *Effayer* or other of his time, a great
Braggard, though but a fmall performer,
and Scandaloufly invective againft his Se-
niours and Superiours ; He handles him
without Mittins, as you may perceive in the
following lines prefented the Vindicator
in lieu of his own Tranfcription.

Lib. 10. Epift. 11.

Nil aliud loqueris quam Thefea, Perithoumq;
  Teque putas Pyladi, Calliodore, Parem.
Difpeream, fi Tu Pyladi preftare matellam
  Dignus es, aut Porcos pafcere Perithoi.

Thou talk'ft of *Thefeus* and of *Perithous*,
And cry'ft, great Pylades is much below us.

Ne're

Ne're let me live, if such a bouncing sott
  Be worthy but to scowr the Chamber-pot
Of *Pylades*, or for a brace of juggs
  To clense the Sties of *Perithous* Hoggs.

This, in brief, since he is pleas'd to remit
the *Observer* to my *Construction*, is all the
Character that I can give of his Works.
For what has *Green tail*, and *Onion-like For-
nicotar* to do with a difference about the
Gamut.   But the Gentleman must be *a la
mode*; For now we can neither plead nor
argue contrary, but the particular lives
and conversations of men must be ravel'd
into, to make slender arguments for weak
Themes, and feeble Causes : A kind of
unmannerly Oratory, that deserves to be
convinc'd rather by Horse-Logick, than by
replies of Pen and Ink.

Page 78. He sayes there is *one scrap of
an Argument* behind yet.   That *these Gentlemen*, meaning the Kings Servants, *attain'd* to their *eminence in Musick* by the
Old Scale.   What fairer Argument would
this great Musitian have, than such a one,
to prove that there is no need of his *Ledger
du main?* If the Scale now in use be a
sufficient *cause*, what need He, or any other
such unskilful Busie-body trouble their
                                             brains

brains whether it be the *Caufa fine qua non*, or no? *'Twere pity*, quo he, *but the Scale were cut in Alablafter*, *and fhew'd among the Tombs*. And 'twere pity, quo I, but His geugaw, B M T, were cut in Paper for Comfit-makers Boxes; or more ferioufly lay'd up among *John Tradefcants* Bawbles. Surely fince thofe Gentlemen he fpeaks of did not attain to their *Eminency* by infpiration, as no queftion but their own Mortality will confefs the contrary; 'tis a very ftrange piece of over-weening rancour in the Vindicatour, to deprive the Poor Harmlefs *Gamut*, of that petty Honour, which is due to the rudiments of all Sciences: Juft like the Mountebank *Pædagogues* about the Town, that will be reviling the ftanch Foundations of Ancient *Lilly*, to ufher in their pedantical lucubrations, and to get themfelves a filly credit in the World, by feeking to cajole the Parents of their Scholars with their own new-fangled Herefies. And all this while, where lyes the ftrefs of fo much *Trinitonian* fury, but only againft the miferable *Ut*, and forlorn *Re?* For *Mi*, *Fa*, *Sol*, *La;* are his white Boys ftill, and admitted into the School-Room to converfe with his young Gentlewomen,

E   B M T

B M T as formerly. Would ye know the reason; on my word 'tis a profound one : For, thinks he, now the *Gamut* is gelt, it may be trusted among Maiden Gentlewomen, which before was somewhat dangerous, when it had the two testicles of *Ut* and *Re*, annexed to it. Though I wonder how B M T themselves scape his lash, there being as much reason why *Base*, *Mean*, and *Treble*, damm'd obsolete Terms of Musick, should suffer the scourge of this Innovating Whipping *Tom*, as *Gam ut* and *A re*.

Therefore might our worthy Vindicator have spar'd his frivolous conceit, that *Those* Gentlemen *came to be no more eminent for having read the Scale*, than the *Macedonian for conquering the World, because his name was Alexander*. An inference that has no more coherence with sense than *Bedlam* with any thing of *Trinity-College* but himself.

'Tis a *Janus*-like fansie, that looks two ways at once ; one part of his Argument rows one way, and the other looks another way ; or to make it yet plainer, as if one Waterman should row one way at the head, and another the quite contrary way at the stern,

ftern, till they pull the Boat in pieces;
which indeed is the true Character of all
the Arguments in his Book. True reason
would have kept him close to his text, and
have told him there was as much likelihood
of *Alexanders* learning the principles of
War, as there was, that the other should
be taught the Rudiments of Musick; so
that if he will grant our Musitians to be
eminent, It will be an easie thing, without
his assistance, to prove that the first ground
and source of their Eminency arose from
their knowledge of the Scale, which is
the first principle of Musick; as we may
well believe the first rise of the *Macedonian*'s greatness was from the great knowledge he had of the first Elements of War;
which being the primary grounds of his
Knowledge, were the primary cause of
that greatness which he attain'd by his
Knowledge. And thus I suppose, the Horn-
book and Primar were the first Originals
of that great learning to which our Vindicator imagins himself to have so sublimely
clamber'd. But this is common sense, and
therefore a thing too mean for him to take
notice of, or else without the verge of his
understanding.

E 2   With

With the fame zealous indifcretion he walks caterwauling, like Pufs upon the Tiles, over another as true a Maxim as any the *Obferver* fets down ; which is, *That the Old Scale is the only Univerfal Character, by which all People of all Nations and Religions converfe in Mufick :* A thing never to be denied, but by the fchifmatical diffonancy of the *Vindicators* ill-bak'd cogitations. For to tell ye that, *becaufe all* Englifh *or* French, *whether they be in* Europe *or* America, *fpeak* Englifh *or* French, therefore *that* French *and* Englifh *are two Univerfal Characters,* is but another refty ftumble of his own illiterate Fancy. The Conclufion it felf, as are all the Conclufions that he makes, is abfolutely falfe and erroneous. For though, for an *Englifhman* or a *Frenchman* to underftand *French* or *Englifh,* nay though each underftood both, render neither of thofe Languages Univerfal , yet when an *Englifh* Mufician fhall by the help of the known Scale, read the Scores of *Italian, French, Spanifh, High-Dutch, Low-Dutch, Polifh, Swedifh,* or of any other Muficians now known in the World ; fhall fing their Songs at firft fight ; play their Airs with the fame nimblenefs ; furely that Character

racter by which they perform all this, muft with the leave of his moft eminent Parts, be accounted pofitively Univerfal.   And therefore for his own ignorance we are neither bound to know, or care to know how to cure it; or if he be blind or cannot fpell, the latter of which is moft likely, 'tis no fault of the *Obfervers*.   In the laft place he lays down five Propofitions, which he advifes the *Obferver*, out of the pride of his filly Heart, to confider before he make himfelf ridiculous;

—— *Dii te*, Damafippe *deæque*
Verum ob confilium donent tonfore ——

But give me leave to tell him, they are not worth an Atome of Confideration, not the leaft thought of a Rag-woman: For the firft and third were things confented to before he had the honour to be born, or the wit to advife; as for the other three, they are but *mendicatory Good your Wor-fhips*, lowfie beggings of the Queftion, the very fame Cony-catching Impoftures, which he has been all this while fo vainly impofing upon the World, for his own pri-vate advantage at *Hackney*, and upon which there has been too much time trifled away already; the Epitome of an idle

Pam·

Pamphlet ; the beginning of which is nothing to the purpose , the middle a very nonsensical piece of Impertinency, and the latter part a parcel of undigested Nonsense, concluded with the grossest brand of Infamy that ever was fix'd upon the *sober* and *ingenuous* Part of the World , whom he so foully accuses to have *entertain'd* such kind *thoughts* of his obnoxious Raillery ; a scandal,which if they forgive him,will bring them within the verge of a most desperate forfeiture : though never to his advantage ; for it will but make the young unwary *Icarus* soar with the more boldness above his understanding , till he melt his Wings, and plunge himself into all the deepest Abysses of Absurdity.

Thus much for *Tobit* , now for his *Little Dog following him.* A certain kind of Letter-Monger, that with much Imprudence, nothing of Truth ; much of Confidence, nothing of Learning ; comes a day after the Fair,to set his *probatum est* to the Mountebankeries of his Master Quack. He was mightily overseen that he did not fix a Label of the Musical Cures wrought by his Benefactor , like a *Covent-Garden Charlatan :* Then might the worshipful Titles
of

of the *Essay* and *Vindication* have been more happily exalted, as frequently they were, by the Induſtrious Stationer, jigg by jowl, with *no Cure no Mony*, or the *Three Infallible Medicines*, upon every poſt of the City, when back'd with ſo many Atteſtations as one of *Melpomene*'s Knights of the Poſt, with a little labour could have eaſily brought him. You may know what part of the Creation he is, by his Braying. This is he that follows the Vindicator, as the Bell-man's Cur follows his Maſter. A kind of Beetle engender'd by the heat of a *Trinity* Meteor, who while the moſt radiant Luminary mov'd in our Hemiſphere, ſlept all the time, but He being ſet in the Ocean of his own Fopperies, up comes this drowſie Inſect, buzzing into your Ears the Vindicators Praiſes; like the Dor-flies, with which the Young Painter in *Boccace* ſo affrighted his Maſter *Bufalmacco*. This is he, who being perhaps as well pay'd for his Letter, as the other was for his Preface, ſtands ready like the Fool in the Play, to juſtifie whatever miſtakes the Vain glorious Squire ſhall be guilty of. I ſhould have expected this Miſerable *Tooter*, with his diminutive Trumpet to have

E 4 ſtood

ftood at the Dore of the *Monſtrous Vindication* to draw in Cuftomers, with a *ſtep in
Gentlemen*; and not to have come fneaking
at the end of a Pamphlet, as if he were
only the Vindicators Excrement, and indeed that very Apocriphal Fart he fpeaks
of, fizzled from the tayl of his own Mufical Pedagogue, and faften'd upon him, as
my Lady puts her fcapes upon *Button*.
You may eafily take the Height of his
Knowledge without a *Jacobs* Staff; for he
tells ye, he has *receiv'd conſiderable advantages* from the *Eſſayer*. This is juſt according
to the Proverb *Aſinus Aſinum ſcabit*.
But now ——

Cedite Romani —— *Cedite Graii* ——

By'r leave, Gentlemen, for a *Hyperbole*,
would make the very Hoops of the Tun of
Heidelbergh flie. *But your Credit*, quoth he,
is too Sacred —— Sure the Vindicator muft
be either a *Nazarite* from his Cradle, or
fome particular vow of feparation to the
Lord; elfe how ridiculoufly looks the
grand and Royal Title of *Sacred* fo un-
decently beftowed upon the low Credit of
a bare Young B M T-monger, and more
in-

indifcreetly fuffer'd by an Oftentatious
Vindicator. But let him write another
Pamphlet, though ne're fo fimple, and
Majefty fhall hardly fuffice him; let him
but add a fourth, and you fhall find N. E.
will make him a God. Well Mr. N. E. I
find you can part with your Commendations at a cheap rate : Though I had
thought, men ought to have valu'd their
Certificates at a higher price, then that of
Herrings and Mackaril. But this it is,
when inconfiderate ftart-ups will be fcrib-
ling, that know not how to guide their
Pens. In my opinion we will allow the
puff'd up Vindicator to take all *N. E's.*
petition'd-for Praifes to himfelf, and make
his beft of them. Let him but wear them
a little in the wind, and he'l foon difcover
the bafenefs of their Metal : For is there
any perfon fo mad, as to think *Sodomy* the
more commendable, beaufe a Cardinal once
wrote in praife of it. However we find
large Commendations given to the Non-
fenfe and arrogance of an *Effay*, and a
more unneceffary and loathfome *Vindication.* Which indeed renders the Com-
mender the greater Impoftor of the two.
Thus they that will undertake to praife
and

and fell their tinfel Wares for right Silver
or Gold, are far greater Cheats than they
who make them for fuch. Men, and Scholars efpecially, that intend their Encomi-
ums fhould be believ'd, fhould confider
whom and what they praife ; and not
with fuch an infipid Prodigality waft the
Jewels of Commendation, as if they were
cafting Beans by peck-fulls to fat Boars.
Such Magnifyings, rather become Dif-
commendations, while the unwary Epiftle-
maker does but baffle his own good In-
tentions to his Friend. So that if any of
the Two, be happy in the Famous *Letter* of
N. E. 'tis the Obferver, while his Reputation grows to be the more notorious, by
the weak endeavour of a frivolous Author
to load him with a heap of paltry Scan-
dals, and empty Forgeries. A lewd ex-
toller, and by confequence a more contemptible difpraifer. 'Tis well known that
the foundnefs, if not profoundnefs of the
Obfervers Judgement and Skill in Mufick,
and the Excellency of his performance favour'd by fo great a Monarch and his
Queen, both whom he ferves in fair re-
pute, are far above the envy of fuch a
Momus as *N. E.* or the hairbrain'd Invention

tion of B M T. And therefore,

Zoile, quid folium fubluto podice perdis?
Spurius ut fiat, Zoile, merge caput.

Neither do I find this Letter-Miffive-Gentleman, teazing only the Obferver; but in his tefty Choler, yerking alfo at *Hudibrafs*, *Rablaife*, and *Don Quixot*, Authors in their kind, whofe Trenchers he is not worthy to fcrape; not without a modicum of invective againft thofe neceffary affiftances of Mufick, *Mood, Time, Prolation*, and *Ligatures of long Notes*; which if Fidlers, and fhallow Compofers have laid afide, are yet fuch *ftrict Obfervances*, as render them of far greater Confequence to a Learned Mufician, than his Epiftolary ignorance is aware of.

If this be one of the *fober and ingenious* part of the World of which the Vindicator brags, He's a fad Mortal, God wot; A miferable Dogger-Boat for fuch a matchlefs Effayer to venture the Shipwrack of his *Sacred Credit* in. A doughty Squire to accompany the Invincible Champion of B M T. Let them e'ne go together with their Mufical Hoop; which if it

ever

ever bring them any advantage, besides that of Pence a piece, for tumbling through, like *Hocus Pocus's*, is past the belief of more of the sober part of the World then I am apt to believe either of them acquainted with.

To

TO
THOMAS SALMON,
M. A. of *Trinity College*, Oxon.
Author of the *Effay to the Advancement of Mufick.*

Sir,

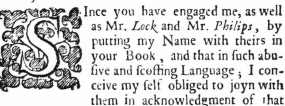Ince you have engaged me, as well as Mr. *Lock* and Mr. *Philips*, by putting my Name with theirs in your Book, and that in fuch abufive and fcoffing Language; I conceive my felf obliged to joyn with them in acknowledgment of that your kindnefs. If my Lines favour not of your Academical Learning, I hope you will excufe me; however, I fhall do my endeavour to write more civilly than you, though in a more homely Stile. The Thanks, Sir, which I intend to return, is only a brief accompt of thofe few Infpections which I have made into your new and elaborate *Effay to the Advancement of Mufick, &c.* with fome fhort Reply's in defence of the Old Scale of Mufick. This being a Work of no great difficulty, I have the more readily and willingly undertaken it; and (for a return of your Favours) fhall make bold to prefent you with thefe my Remarques.

Firft, Before your Title Page appears the Picture
of

of a Fine young Lady (of Mufical Education in *Hackney* School no doubt) Playing and Singing to her Lute. 'Twas excellent policy to fix fuch a fair Bait there, for it will moft certainly catch both the Eyes and Hearts of all our new foft-headed Gallants; and undoubtedly draw more Spectators to your Book than ever Merry *Andrew* did to his Mafter *Jacob Halls* Stage.

Next is the Title, or a Defcription of what is held forth in your Book, in as many large promifing Words and Truths, as there is in thofe Mountebank Doctors Bills; which are pafted up at every piffing Corner; (and it was ingeniously done of your Stationer Mr. *Car* to pafte your Title alfo in the fame places, fince they do fo well correfpond;) 'tis in thefe words, *An Effay to the Advancement of Mufick, by cafting away the perplexity of different Cliffs, and uniting all forts of Mufick, Lute, Viol, Violin, Organ, Harpfichord, Voice,* (with *&c.* to include all other kinds, as Bagpipes, Jews-trump, Drums, Trumpets, Tongs, *&c.*) *in one Univerfal Character.* And that we might not think this Work defigned by a mean or obfcure Perfon, it follows, *By* THOMAS SALMON, *Mafter of Arts of* Trinity College *in* Oxford. But how well this is made out by you in your following Difcourfe, I leave to the judgment of all ingenious Muficians.

In the following Page is an Epiftle by Mr. *John Birchenfha*, your Publifher, no mean Perfon in the Science of Mufick, witnefs his Learned *Templum Muficum*, and this his Epiftle, or *Flambeau*, to Light all Muficians out of their *Egyptian* Darknefs,

nefs, to behold the *New Light* or *Mufical Elyfium*
held forth in your *Effay* : And this Commendatory
Epiftle is fo fubtlely and plaufibly done, to the
Advancement of your new Reformation, that he
deferves double the Reward he received for it. It
begins thus : *There is not any Art, which at this*
day is more Rude, Unpolifh'd, and Imperfect in the
Writings of the Ancient and Modern Authors, than
Mufick; for the Elementary part thereof, is little
better than an indigefted Mafs, and confufed Chaos
of impertinent Characters, and infignificant Signs.
It is intricate and difficult to be underftood ; it afflicts
the Memory, and confumeth much time, before the
knowledge thereof can be attained : Becaufe the
Cliffs are divers; their Tranfpofitions frequent ; the
Order and places of Notes very mutable; and their
denominations alterable and unfix'd. Thefe things
being confidered by the ingenious Author of this Book,
(who endeavoureth only a reformation of the Regula-
tive Principles of Practical Mufick) he hath here
prefented thee with an Eexpedient, for the redrefs of
thefe Obftacles, &c.

Now, Sir, you being that ingenious Author here
mentioned, which has by your elaborate Pains,
great Learning, and fubtle Invention, found out this
new Expedient or Reformation, I fhall leave the
Publifher and Epiftle, and proceed to examin the
feveral Particulars and great Advantages propofed
to us by your Book.

The firft Chapter is nothing to the purpofe of
Reformation, but a bare Difcourfe of the Advantages of Mufick, which is frequent in all Authors
that have written of that Science.

The

The second Chapter is entituled, *The Gamut Reform'd:* Here the Axe is laid to the Root, and you begin your Reformation thereof in words of reproach and defamation, thus : *That which first of all terrifies a Beginner, is a long Discourse of Gibbrish, a fardle of hard Names and fictitious Words, called the* Gamut, *presented to him perfectly to be learned without Book, till he can readily repeat it backwards and forwards; as though a man must be exact in the Art of Conjuring before he might enter upon Musick.* Are not these prety Bugbear Words, to fright Boys and Girls ever from learning Musick by such a *Gamut*, that is compounded of hard infignificant Words to Conjure up Devils? This, Sir, shews, that because you understand not the excellent Use of that *Gamut*, and its Words or Names, you are therefore offended with it, and endeavour to perswade others to the same opinion with your self, which is ever the practice of Innovators. Certainly, Sir, Men of greater knowledge in the Science of Musick than you can pretend to, have declared them of better Use; who tell us, That they are Words or Names, by which Notes or Sounds are called and known in their distinct and proper places; and Notes or Sounds comprehend Musick, and Musick is known rather to expel Devils than raise them; it did out of *Saul*, but, Sir, what operation it may have upon you, I know not. You go on in these Words, *But I am certain if he can say,* G, A, B, C, D, E, F, G, *it will do to all intents and purposes* [*as well*]. We thank you for this *as well*, but, Sir, will it do no better? then why do you propose it to us, when there's no advantage in it?

Are

Are we not much beholding to you, Sir, to deprive us of our Old Scale, which is Universally approved, and by known experience found to be perfect and good. And impose upon us this New one of your own production, lame and deformed, a thin-gut Monster, which has neither Speech nor Language, whereby it may be understood ; yet are you so in love with it, that you would fain lick it into some kind of form : But your Tongue (though well hung) is not long enough.

Your next words are these, *For the plain truth is, there are but seven Notes in all, only repeated over and over again in double and treble proportion.* You say very right, Sir, but this is demonstrated more plain in the Old Scale than in your New one, as thus it appears : In the Old Scale the seven Notes and their Names are repeated three times over in words at length, on their proper and assigned Rules and Spaces : In yours but once, and that in single Letters only ; which you tell us is to be done over and over in double and treble proportions. Surely this needs must confound a Beginner, there being no plain demonstration to guide him, but only your Eight single Letters, and his own Imagination.

Page 14. your words are these, *Those aforesaid hard Names are nothing to the purpose, they can't declare a Note to be in a different Octave.* This declares again, that you do not, or wilfully will not understand the Old Scale, notwithstanding Mr. *Locke* lately sent you an excellent pair of Observing Spectacles for that purpose, with which if you view the Old Scale, you will see there are different names enough in each of the Octaves, to di-

F   stinguish

ſtinguiſh them in their proper places of *Baſs*, *Mean*, and *Treble*. Is not the Octave to *Gam ut* in the *Baſs G ſol re ut* in the *Mean*? To *A re*, *A la mi re*; To *B mi*, *B fab mi*; To *C fa ut*, *C ſol fa ut*; To *D ſol re*, *D la ſol re*? Here are diverſe Names ſufficient to diſtinguiſh between the Octaves of the *Baſs* and *Mean*. So in the *Treble*, or higher Octave there are differeit Names, as *C ſol fa*, *D la ſol*, *E la*; which Names are in neither of the lower Octaves of *Mean* and *Baſs*. Therefore this Objection againſt the Old Scale is removed, and may be fixed more properly upon your New one, which confiſts only of Eight ſingle Letters, ſet down in this Chap. Page 17. and there named The *New Gamut* : So that all a Beginner hath to diſtinguiſh your Octaves by, is to ſay *A* in the firſt, and *A* in the ſecond, and *A* in the third, which is the whole deſign of your — what d'ye call't — Hypotheſis, or circulation of Octaves; and probably might hold good, if all that learn'd your way, were taught to Sing by Letters, or Tablature; for by Notes they cannot: And this it was which made you ſcratch your head to the purpoſe. But what will not a man do, before he will ſcratch a hole in't : Alaſs, your New *Gamut* is ſo young, it can't ſpeak, nor ever would, unleſs you ſeek out for help; wherefore, rather than it ſhould continue ſpeechleſs, you'l take confidence, and borrow out of the Old Scale thoſe Gibbriſh Words or Names of Notes, *Sol La Mi Fa*, *&c.* which but a little before you render ſo terrible to a Learner. He that ſhall read your Page 15. will have cauſe to ſmile to hear how ridiculouſly you

quar-

quarrel againſt the Old Scale ; yet in the four laſt
Lines thereof your words are theſe —— *Wherefore*
that We may know how to place Mi, *They give us this*
Rule, (not ſo, for you take it) *which alwayes holds*
good , (a civil acknowledgment) viz. *before* Mi *aſ-*
cending to name Fa Sol La , *and after* Mi *deſcen-*
ding La Sol Fa.

Now Sir , you have gotten this Old Rule, I will
inſert your following words in the next Page , that
it may appear to all Judicious perſons what a prety
confuſion you make about ordering them for the
Mouth of your *New Gamut.*

Now that which they are to be blamed for in this is ,
that when they have given their Scholars a Notional
underſtanding of this direction , their practice is to
take their riſe from Sol, *and Sing* Sol La Mi Fa Sol
La Fa Sol ; *as though* Sol *was the ſyllable from*
whence they ſhould take aim, by which means they never
perfect their main rule, and ſo as Mi *alters , are con-*
founded in naming their Notes ; whereas, if in their
practice they begin with Mi, *and ſo Sing forwards ,*
Mi Fa Sol La Fa Sol La Mi, *they would at once learn*
to riſe an Octave with their Voice , and gain a rea-
dineſs in this Rule, which they are always to account
by in whatſoever condition they find Mi.

It is to no purpoſe to plead that Sol *is for the moſt*
part in the Cliff *line , and therefore ready to begin*
with as they go upward ; becauſe theſe ſyllables are
practiced only in order to other Singing ; now Songs
begin not with Sol, *and go forward in that method ,*
but upon any Note, and ſo skip about , that no Rule
can be obſerved, but that which we contend for alway₅
to be practiſed.

This is indeed the language of your whole Book,
(as it will appear to fuch as fhall read it) 'tis fuch a
Babel of confufion, Fardle of contradictions, and
Impoffibilities : Such a Mathematical Rat-Trap of
Non-fenfe , as the like was never made in *Crooked-
Lane.* In the former Chapter you confine the
Notes, here the Names', and fet them in the Stocks
together ; as appears by thefe your next words,
Page 18.

*We are fure, what we have undertook, is fufficiently
proved , that* G, A, B, C, D, E, F, G, *will do as well
as the old hard Names* ; *and for the placing of* Mi *,
you muft take the ufual Monofyllables , fo you order
them in the moft practicable method, viz* Mi Fa
Sol la Fa Sol La Mi.

So that here *Mi* is always in your firft line *G* ,
Fa in *A*, *Sol* in *B*, and *La* in *C* ; and fo afcending
in your firft Octave , you begin *Mi* again in the
fecond : All by way of Circulation.

And fo again in the 2cth Page of your *Vindication*, your words are thefe , *How happy would it be
for the eafe of Mufick , and the exactnefs of Tuning,
if the fame proportions were ever fixed to the fame
places of the eptenary* (or your Octaves) *i. e.* Mi
alwayes in B. And again, in Page 49. *And about
the confinement of* Mi *with the avoiding regular* flats
and fharps, *I have delivered my Judgement in the
Defcription of my Whirligig :* (That is your Cart
Wheel with Seven Spokes :) The firft beginning in
Mi and as it makes a turn round , it comes to *Mi*
again. So that all you give us for a New
Gamut , is your Whirligig , or Wheel of feven
Spokes, marked with *G A B C D E F* , which you
fay

fay is a fpeedier way to attain Mufick then to take a long Journey on foot by the Old *Gamut*. And fince your neareft way to it is the furtheft about, let thofe that ike it take it, and your fecond Chapter to boot : I have done with it. If this won't do, I have yet more in Vindication of the Old Scale of *Mufick*.

I come next to your Third Chapter, (in which and the former is contained your whole Defign) Entitled *The Cliffs reduced to one Univerfal Charaĉter*. The firft Page or it is nothing to the purpofe, but a fardle or words about *Tablature, &c*. But in the middle of your next page your words are thefe, *The prefent Practice* (or Old Way) *is to make three Cliffs, whofe Notes by which they are called, are a Fifth above one another ; and according to the moft conveniency in writing, are ufually affigned to there places, as in the Scheme*.

And fince you have done us the kindnefs to infert a Scheme of our three Cliffs, in your Book , (which you borrow'd out of Mr. *Simpfon's Compendium*, Page 4. as you do all your other Examples from him and other men) I doubt not to prove that your new Invented Cliffs B M T will B℮-℮MpTy of any Invention you pretend to the Advancement of *Mufick*.

An Example of the Three proper Cliffs affigned to each Part.

Bafs.   Mean.   Treble.

By these Three Cliffs, as they are thus planted in there usual and proper places, may be Prick'd any Song proper for that Part, and in the compass of the Voice, and without any transposition (except it be in the *C sol fa ut* Cliff) which is vniversally proper to the inward or middle Parts, and is so transposed sometimes for conveniency of Pricking, especially in Cathedral Musick, where Anthems and Services of five and six Parts do require it: Nor doth the transposition of that Cliff create any confusion to a Beginner, as you *vainly* alledge; for Vocal Musick is seldom learn'd by men of Forty or Fifty Years old, but by those that are young, whose Voyces are proper to the *Treble*, and by that Cliff are only taught; nor is the *C sol fa ut* Cliff now much used (unless as I said before) in Cathedral Musick. If you cast your Eye upon those several Collections of Ayres and Songs, which I have lately published, you will find I have not made use of the *C sol fa ut* Cliff in all the second Part of the *Musical Companion*, which consists of Songs of Two, Three and Four Parts; but Printed them all in the *G*, or *Treble* Cliff, as proper to be Sung by Men or Boys. As to my *Psalms* in Four Parts, which are Printed in three *Tenor* Cliffs and a *Bass*; I could have Printed them as well in Three *Treble* Cliffs, had I thought all had been so ignorant in the use of our Cliffs as I am assured you are. It being usual and common for Men to Sing those Songs which are prick'd in a *Treble* an Eighth Lower, where the Parts are so Composed, that they do not interfere with the *Bass*. And if Musick be made difficult (as you say) by the
transs-

tranfpofition of one of our Cliffs, I fhall plainly demonftrate that you have made it ten times more difficult and confufed, by the frequent tranfpofition of your Three new invented Cliffs B M T, in your new whim-wham Circulation of Octaves; which according to your Hypothefis is thus fet down in your Diagram.

Bafs.   *Mean.*   *Treble.*

In Page 38 and 39 you give us thefe following Rules and Directions, *viz.* 1. *In any place, where the Notes rife or fall an Octave (which is ufually the caufe of greateft diftrefs in this cafe) fet the next Note in the fame place, only changing the letter of the Octave, which will direct you to Sing it an eighth higher or lower; as you may fee thefe three Notes, which required three different Places, in three different Cliffs, are here fituated all upon the fame Line, only with the letters of their Octaves prefix'd at firft fight, palpably difcovering what they ftand for.*

By which means the Octave only, not the Cliff is altered, neither is there the leſt ſhadow of the old confufion; for the G, *which I inſtanced in, or any other Note in this cafe, will ſtand in every part in the fame place. And certainly, one that has but very indifferent skill in Singing, can rife or fall an Octave, when the prefixed letter fhall give him timely warning of it.* 2. *If the Notes afcend, or defcend by degrees, and you have occafion to go far into anothr*

Octave

Octave, when you come to an higher G, *alter the Signal Letter, and it falls upon the lowermost Line* ; *the like discretion also must be used in descending : By which means, and good fore-cast, no Song can be so spiteful and unlucky, but may be evidently and conveniently written in the compass of four Lines, which is the* STATUTE OF OUR HYPOTHESIS, *the lowermost beginning with* G, *the uppermost ending with* F ; *and the higher and lower Notes than these, by the change of the Signal Letter ought to be lodged in their own Octaves to which they do belong.*

Hitherto I hope, Sir, I have proceeded fairly ; and because it shall appear so, I will here, according to this *Statute of your Hypothesis*, give one or two Examples of both together, and leave it to Judicious Judgements to determine where the confusion, or transposition of Cliffs is most frequent, and which is most pleasant to the Eye of the Learner.

An Example according to the Rule of the Old Gamut, *wherein the whole Scale is Prick'd down proper for Vocal Musick, in two Cliffs only,* viz. *the Bass and Treble* ; *in which compass may be Prick'd any Song without any transposition.*

Example.

The same your New Way is thus,

A common Tune of a Psalm, prick'd according to the Old Rule or Scale of Musick.

The same Tune Prick'd your Way.

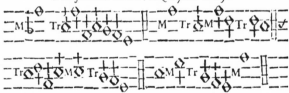

Now behold, good Sir, is not this Tune prickt according to the STATUTE of your *Hypothesis* or new Method you would impose upon us? I am sure it is. In our way there is no Transposition of Cliffs, but in yours, in this short Tune of Twenty eight Notes, your M T Cliffs are Transpos'd or Impos'd no less than Eleven times; and are not the

Notes

Notes cunningly planted for a Beginner to *Sol-Fa*?
'Tis so retrograde to our old Rule, that when our
Notes Rise your Notes Fall, and when ours Fall
yours Rise, to the Eye. Had I not heard otherwise,
I should have imagined you had been a *Quaker*, you
so imitate them, who act all by contraries, against
the established Rule both in Church and State; for
because our Three Cliffs, *Bass*, *Mean*, and *Treble*,
are distinguished by three known Characters out of
the Old Scale, your Three Cliffs must be otherwise, *B* for *Bass*, *M* for *Mean*, and *Tr* for *Treble*:
An excellent Reformation! and to as much purpose,
as he that changed the Name *Kingdom* into *Common-
wealthdom*.

But I cannot find, Sir, in all your new *Essay* any
provision for *Tenors* and *Contratenors*; you never
thought of Cathedral Men, which are the greatest
number of Singers in the Land; sure your design
is, that since you cann't do as the late Reformers did,
sequester them of their Means, you will sequester
them of their Musical Cliffs, *Tenors* and *Contratenors:* For this, I remember Mr. *Lock* gave you a
Check in his *Observations*, and wondred you could
be so *uncivil:* To which (in the 49*th* Page of your
Vindication) you answer, *If he still grumbles that
Scholars cann't tell which is a Contratenor, or lower
Mean, or the like, for them that cann't understand
the nature of the thing; let there be writ over them,
This is a Cock, and that is a Bull; which I take to
be an easier remedy than to learn all the variety of old
Cliffs.* From whence (according to your method)
I may draw this Inference, That the Gentlemen of
His Majesties Chappel, and all Cathedral Singing-
men,

men, are prefented by you (for the *Advancement*
of their *Mufick*) with little better than a Story of
a C O C K and a B U L L ; for which I fhall leave
them to give you thanks, and proceed further in the
Vindication of our Cliffs.

Since all your whole Defign, Sir, is to have
Mufick confin'd, and kept to the *Statute Rule* of
your *Hypothefis*, which is by three *Octaves* fix'd
to conftant Kules and Spaces, in the compafs of
Four Lines, for the Pricking of all Songs; why
did you not give us fome Examples thereof in your
Book, but tell us, *That no Song can be fo fpightful
or unlucky, but it may be evidently and conveniently
written in the compafs of Four Lines, by the Rule of
OUR Hypothefis:* Your omiffion in this cafe, gave
me occafion to infert the foregoing Tune of a
Pfalm; I could have prick'd down many more (but
this may fuffice any ingenious perfon)to have fhewed
you the Beauty of the Miftrefs of your Invention ; but
I fuppofe you perceived by her limping and hop-
ping what was her Diftemper, which made you pre-
fcribe her a *Leiger-Line*, and if that would not
perfect the Cure, then to add thereto an *afcititious
Line*, which together would prove an Infallible
Remedy for the Rickettinefs of your dearly Beloved B M T, and no doubt enable her to walk
in the fame path and ftate with the *Old Scale:*
For though in many places you plead hard for the
keeping to the *Statute* of your *Hypothefis*, *viz.* Four
Lines, as for inftance, in *pag.* 73. your words are
thefe, *But left any one fhould ftill run droaning in his
own way, I fhall mind him of OURS, and tell him
again, WE do not reckon upwards, as if the Lines*
were

were continued together ; neither make WE any Cliffs
five Notes afunder , but WE compleat an Octave in
the Syfteme of Four Lines , which reaches to F fa ut,
and then begin the Syfteme of the next Four Lines in
the Middle Part with G *again* ; *as after* Saturday
night comes Sunday *morning :* Or to explain your
meaning, 'tis thus ; after you have gone up feven
Rounds of the Ladder, you muft come down again
to the firft to go the eighth : Yet notwithftanding
this, you tell us before in *pag.* 23. of certain Notes
which you call *Pilgrim Notes , that have higher and*
lower fteps to go , and will not be fix'd in any conftant
dwellings (now for thefe in your next words are
fome Crums of Comfort, for you have provided
them Lodgings let them ramble whether they pleafe)
but that the following Contrivance fhows me it may ,
and is here already accomplifhed Welcome Leiger-
Line. Handy-pandy, now, fhall we have a Leiger-
Line, or no Leiger Line ? You refolve this doubt in
the aforefaid *pag.* 73. when you tell us, *If for con-*
veniency of Pricking , WE *allow the Syfteme to be*
of [*Five*] *or* [*Six*] *Lines , &e.* Rejoice O ye
Mufical Notes, here's a Gaol-delivery ! you fhall
be no longer confin'd in the Prifon of a Four-Line
Hypothefis. But till this was done, Sir, your
Mrs. *Aurelia,* with her Song of Four Parts, could
not appear ; which you tell us, *pag.* 82. Mr. *Theod.*
Stefkins tranfcribed for you ; I wonder, fince you
were not capable of doing it your felf, you did not
require the affiftance of your *Publifher* in that as
well as in all the reft : In *pag.* 37. where this Song
is fix'd as an Example , that it may be done your
Five-line way, and not in your Four-line way, your
words

words are thefe; *But that you may fee how unnecef-sary thofe former various Cliffs are, how conveniently a Song will fall in the Syfteme of Five Lines, for though an Octave is compleated in Four, yet you may take fuch a liberty, &c.* Therefore, Sir, that you may fee we can prefent you with this Song in lefs various Cliffs than you have done, I have tranfcribed it in the fame Key you have put it in, that when it is compared with yours, the World may judge wherein lies the Advantages you propofe.

A. 4. Voc.   Mr. *Pelham Humphryes.*

When *Aurelia, &c.*

I have but one Example more, by which may be judged now you have got a Leger Line to make Five as well as we, whether you be not almost come back into our Old Way of Pricking, as well as you did before into the use of the Words of our *Gamut*.

The

The Old way.

Unisons in their proper places.

Unisons in their proper places.

Your New way.

Unisons out of their proper places.

Unisons out of their proper places.

By this Example I prove your *Univerfal Chara-Eter* of having *G* always on the Firft Line to be con-fufed, whatever pretences and plaufible words you give us to the contrary: For to make the fame Note to be in two places at one time (in the Space in the *Bafs* and on the Rule in the *Mean*) is to fit between two Stools, whereby the A— of your whole Defign will fall to the ground. If you could have kept to your firft firſt Rule of Four-line Octaves, you had committed that abſurdity but once, and that in your Octave Note only, but now by your Leiger-Lines you advance it in as many Notes as you pleaſe; whereas on the contrary, you may ſee our Uniſons of the *Baſs* when they come into the *Mean*, are, if in Space in Space, if on Rule on Rule, and the like 'twixt the *Mean* and *Treble*. By all which it will appear, that our *Gamut* is a perfect Rule, and ſo are our Cliffs in their uſe, without any difficulty or confuſion, how ridiculouſly and ignorantly ſoever you have rendred them.

Thus far I have Vindicated the *Old Scale*; I could have enlarged much further, but as I turn'd over both your *Eſſay* and *Vindication*, I met with ſo many impertinent Impoſſibilities and Contradictions, eſpecially about Inſtrumental Muſick, ſo confuſedly jumbled together; and not finding the *Gittar* (the only School-Inſtrument) ſo much as mentioned in all your Book, and your *Hypotheſis* being ſo pertinent to it; I had not patience, but threw them aſide, as unworthy the peruſal of any Perſon skill'd in Muſick.

Sir,

Auguſt 26.
1672.　　　Your humble Servant in any thing

but your new Muſical HYPOTHESIS,

John Playford.

F I N I S.